Praise for

Walking with Sam

A Barnes & Noble Best Book of 2023

"[A] good setup for a travel memoir, ripe with opportunities to revisit the past and measure his own faded youth against the full flourishing of his son's young adulthood. And McCarthy—who wrote about his Brat Pack years in a previous memoir—makes the most of them."
—*New York Times Book Review*

"I greatly enjoyed this father-and-son saunter for its fractiousness and sulks, exasperation and blisters, and ultimately its harmony and resolution, proving the saying *solvitur ambulando*—'It is solved by walking.'"
—Paul Theroux

"In candid detail and deftly written prose, the book recounts the duo's conversations (on everything from the profound to the mundane), their struggles (typically spurred by heat-related exhaustion), and the friends they made along the way. It is as much a travel memoir as a reflection on parenting, as McCarthy aims to better understand and bond with his son, who is on the cusp of adulthood."
—Shondaland.com

"McCarthy shares exquisite details of their surroundings, providing historical context.... The process of the two connecting over time is heartwarming and relatable.... A sweet gem of a tale that will appeal to McCarthy fans and those who appreciate a challenging journey."
—*Library Journal*

"The trail is blisteringly hot and dusty, and in villages along the way, the two encountered surly waiters, bad food, and inadequate places to stay. The walk, though, was never about the destination but rather about a father and son readying themselves for a new stage in their lives."

—*Kirkus Reviews*

"McCarthy's depiction of the rewarding endeavor of walking the Camino with his son is both worthwhile and entertaining." —*Booklist*

"In this compelling book, McCarthy walks five hundred miles across Spain's Camino de Santiago with his eldest son, Sam. This narrative is intimate, witty, engaging, and poignant." —*Digital Journal*

Walking with Sam

Also by Andrew McCarthy

The Longest Way Home

Just Fly Away

Brat

Walking with Sam

A Father, a Son, and Five Hundred Miles across Spain

Andrew McCarthy

GRAND
CENTRAL

New York   Boston

Grand Central Publishing
Hachette Book Group
1290 Avenue of the Americas, New York, NY 10104
grandcentralpublishing.com
@grandcentralpub

Originally published in hardcover and ebook by Grand Central Publishing in May 2023
First trade paperback edition: May 2024

Grand Central Publishing is a division of Hachette Book Group, Inc. The Grand Central Publishing name and logo is a trademark of Hachette Book Group, Inc.

The publisher is not responsible for websites (or their content) that are not owned by the publisher.

The Hachette Speakers Bureau provides a wide range of authors for speaking events. To find out more, go to hachettespeakersbureau.com or email HachetteSpeakers@hbgusa.com.

Grand Central Publishing books may be purchased in bulk for business, educational, or promotional use. For information, please contact your local bookseller or the Hachette Book Group Special Markets Department at special.markets@hbgusa.com.

Library of Congress Cataloging-in-Publication Data

Names: McCarthy, Andrew, 1962– author.
Title: Walking with Sam : a father, a son, and five hundred miles across Spain / Andrew McCarthy.
Description: First edition. | New York : Grand Central Publishing, 2023.
Identifiers: LCCN 2022057862 | ISBN 9781538709207 (hardcover) | ISBN 9781538757086 | ISBN 9781538757093 | ISBN 9781538709221 (ebook)
Subjects: LCSH: McCarthy, Andrew, 1962—Family. | McCarthy, Sam. | Actors—United States—Biography. | Fathers and sons—United States—Biography. | Camino de Santiago de Compostela. | LCGFT: Autobiographies.
Classification: LCC PN2287.M5446 A3 2023 | DDC 791.4302/8092 [B]—dc23/eng/20221213
LC record available at https://lccn.loc.gov/2022057862

ISBNs: 9781538709214 (trade paperback), 9781538709221 (ebook)

Printed in the United States of America

CW

10 9 8 7 6 5 4 3 2 1

For my father

Camino de Santiago
Camino Frances

Santiago
de Compostela

Sarria

72
miles

162
miles

Astorga

Leon

192
miles

Sahagún

228
miles

St. Jean
Pied de Port

439
miles

Pamplona

380
miles

Burgos

Logroño

304
miles

Prologue

When I was a very young man and became very successful in the movies very quickly, I harbored a notion that I had not earned my accomplishments, that I hadn't done the requisite work, that it was all merely a fluke, that I didn't deserve it. When a magazine article linking me to a group of other young actors branded us spoiled, fame-seeking punks called the Brat Pack appeared, this internal sensitivity was matched by outward perception. I was someone who skimmed, who bypassed the effort and claimed the rewards. A lightweight. Whether any of this contained truth is debatable, but that it burrowed under my skin and became my adopted perception of myself there is little doubt.

Walking across the Camino de Santiago a quarter century ago challenged all that. It hadn't been my conscious intent to reclaim the narrative of my own life, yet that's what happened. Whereas I had become someone who reacted to events, deflecting what felt like attacks, dodging emotional entanglements, grasping at what seemed to be diminishing opportunities, my time in Spain planted seeds for another way to perceive things, and gave me an internal baseline from which to go forth in the world. Simply because I started walking. I walked. And walked. Across a country. For five weeks and five hundred miles. It was something that could not be taken away or be easily dismissed, even by me. I earned my way across Spain.

Each day during the walk I was reminded of this by the town churches—although not for the obvious reasons. When a pilgrim is still out among the wheat and dust and a long way off from any village, the first sign of civilization that will often appear on the horizon is a church spire—the highest point in the town. I always felt a mix of relief and fatigue upon seeing those spires. "My God, that's still so far away," I always thought. Invariably the walk into the village was quicker and easier than I had first perceived. And I had done it. On my own. There had been no shortcuts.

Years later, after I no longer viewed myself as a person who skimmed and cut corners, but rather was someone who merited his successes and could swallow his failures, I was able to attribute the first sense of earning what I had achieved and who I had become back to those church spires. There was something in the walking that had burned marrow-deep, into a knowing that couldn't be shaken.

For so long I had felt ill-equipped, insufficient in some way, and often very alone. It took the Camino to teach me that I was solid in myself. It was the greatest of the many gifts it gave me and something I wish I'd learned much earlier. It's time to pass that gift on. So after a quarter century I've returned to northern Spain—and I've brought my son.

Part 1

It requires a direct dispensation from heaven to become a walker.

—*Henry David Thoreau*

"I am about to get so sick of you"

484 miles to Santiago

The glass doesn't just break, it explodes into hundreds, thousands, of pieces. On the terrace, under a glow of artificial light in the summer night, Sam and I are getting up to leave the café off the central square of Place Charles de Gaulle in the Basque village of Saint-Jean-Pied-de-Port in the southwest of France at the base of the Pyrenees Mountains when his hand brushes against the goblet. Over the course of his nineteen years, my son has tipped sippy cups, dropped juice boxes, spilled glasses of milk, dumped soda, upended energy drinks, overflowed celebratory champagne flutes. "It wouldn't be Thanksgiving if Sam didn't knock over a glass," his younger sister, Willow, once remarked after Sam sent his water flying over the turkey. Often these mishaps are a source of amusement—just as often they're not.

On this evening, I react with a flash of anger—I recognize this as a manifestation of my anxiety over the trip we are about to embark upon. This emotion is stifled. Embarrassment bubbles up as I feel the heads of neighboring diners begin to turn. I ease into a laugh of recognition. This chain reaction of feelings occurs in less than a second. When I meet Sam's eye, his mouth is agape, his expression is one of surprise, familiar resignation, a plea to me for leniency, and a whimsical acceptance of who he is, all at once.

I go inside to tell the waiter what happened. The mustachioed man reaches for a small dustpan and hand sweep. I suggest he's going to need

5

a bigger boat. He looks at me and I nod gravely. He goes for the large push broom.

We had landed in Bilbao, Spain, hours earlier. While in the air, Sam's mom and my former wife, Carol, had sent me a text. "You wanted to take this trip together before Sam was even walking," she wrote. "Enjoy! (And take some Band-Aids for the blisters.)"

"Mom texted, wishing us luck," I said as we hauled our rucksacks off the baggage carousel. "Did you bring Band-Aids, by the way?"

"That's your job, bro."

A taxi carried us over an invisible border into France, and in the lingering light deposited us in front of a small hotel. The door was locked. I called the number taped to the glass, and in time a sour young man with the bearing of someone twice his age admitted us and assigned us our room. Upstairs, I took a quick look and hurried back down the flight of stairs to the desk before the clerk vanished again.

"We need two beds," I told him in my bad Spanish (we were in France). "I made a reservation for a room with two beds."

He stared at me. "There are two beds," he said in English.

Back upstairs, Sam had thrown his backpack down and was lying beside it on the queen bed. Next to the door, somehow unnoticed by me in my haste to ensure everything was in order, was a small twin bed.

"Where'd you go?" Sam asked.

"Um..." I was tempted to lie to my son.

The Camino de Santiago is well known to illuminate fears, doubts, and insecurities of pilgrims who decide to make the walk. My own experience on The Way long ago confirms this. But we haven't even started yet! Already a vague and long-held dread about some innate parenting skill I fear I lack is raising its head. And there's the lingering sense of insufficient manhood I've harbored for even longer. Maybe on this trip all my deficiencies will be exposed—my son will recognize me for a fraud, a failure, a weakling. Maybe this was all my own father's fault. Maybe this walk was a terrible idea. Maybe I was just hungry.

"I didn't see the other bed," I confessed.

"What?"

"I didn't notice this bed."

Sam looked up from his phone. "You gotta chill, bro."

I crossed the room and flung open the wooden shutters. Down below was the cobbled, medieval Rue de la Citadelle. The Camino. For twenty-six years I promised myself I'd see it again. I had begun to doubt that I would keep that promise. It seemed that time might take away something I knew to be important, and age would have to justify its loss. But life, it now appeared, had been waiting for the right circumstance.

Our walk of five hundred miles would begin here and lead us over the Pyrenees, out of France into the Basque region of Spain to Pamplona, through the wine country of La Rioja, the city of Burgos, then out onto the treacherous high Meseta, onward to the bustle of León, and into the verdant hills of Galicia, ending in the far west of Iberia at the Cathedral in Santiago de Compostela, a little over a month later—if all went well.

"Let's get some dinner," I said to Sam. "Before the restaurants close."

"We just got here, bro," my son replied from the bed, staring at his phone.

"You're not in New York now, Sammy. Things close."

"Okay."

He didn't move.

"Come on, let's go. I'm hungry."

"Oh my God, I am about to get so sick of you."

I first seriously broached the idea of this walk to Sam several months earlier, at home in Manhattan. I was cleaning up after dinner. My eldest son entered the kitchen.

"Want to go for a walk, Sam?"

"A walk? Why?"

"Thought it might be a nice idea."

"Not really."

"Okay."

Sam left the kitchen. A few minutes later, he called out from the living room, "Where?"

"Spain," I shouted back.

Sam reentered the kitchen. "Spain?"

"Yeah."

"I thought you meant like to the deli to get paper towels or something."

"No."

"For how long?" he asked.

"About a month, five weeks."

"You mean on the Camino?"

"I do."

There was a long pause. Then, "Yeah, I'll do that."

I stifled my delight.

Then he added quickly, "But not right now. I got stuff going on."

And there the idea sat. Until I got a call one recent afternoon.

"Everything OK, Sammy?" I answered. For the past year and a half, the "stuff" Sam had "going on" was his first serious romantic relationship—until it all came crashing down. The breakup, I knew, was sudden and severe and devastating.

"Dad, if you still want to go do that walk," my boy mumbled into the phone, "I'll go."

"Yeah?"

"Yeah, sure." He sounded exhausted. "Whatever."

I knew from my own experience that a call for help can come in the most disinterested of tones. I walked to the living room, opened my computer, and bought two plane tickets.

Days later, here we are.

The morning air is cool, fog hangs in the valley. Eager to get started, I'm looking down from our window again. I see a half dozen or more men and women, a few alone, others in pairs, all laden with packs, moving along the narrow lane toward the Porte d'Espagne, the stone archway at the bottom of the Rue de la Citadelle, which leads out of town, across the River Nive, and up into the mountains. Walkers on the road to Santiago tend to get an early start—most are on the hoof by 7:00 a.m., many before dawn. It's after eight. I still can't get Sam out of the bathroom.

He shouts through the door, "Should I wear the same underwear I have on?"

The eldest of my three children is on the threshold of manhood and an independent life.

"Do you need me to make these decisions, Sam?" I call back. Sam has typically not needed or even allowed such hands-on parenting as he is currently seeking. Long gone are the days when I had the power to make him happy simply with my attention and affection. (I still have this pleasure with my youngest, Rowan.)

Our relationship has been much closer than mine was with my father, when, at seventeen, I left home and never looked back. Yet, perhaps because of my own history, I've always harbored a dread that a similar parting between Sam and me was preordained.

It didn't help that when Sam was deeply involved in his relationship with The Ex, it seemed that overnight he had left us. Suddenly gone were the evenings when he would march into our bedroom unannounced, pace at the foot of Dolores's and my bed, rehash his day or make proclamations on why school was a waste of his time, or share unsolicited insights into how I might better have handled an earlier interaction with his sister, Willow. Lately, Dolores and I just turned out the light.

I understood this evolution to be typical, normal, even appropriate behavior as the young discover love and sex and begin to carve out their own lives. But on yet another day when Sam entered and passed through the house and then out again without even grunting a greeting while his girlfriend waited mute by the door, Dolores turned to me: "So is Sam just gone from our lives now?" It hit me hard that my active relationship with my son might already be over.

As a young man—like many young men—I never thought of myself becoming a parent. But that I love my kids beyond my comprehension makes me no different from nearly all those who have children. And if you were to ask me by what yardstick I would measure my life a success, the reply would be that if all my children desire a close relationship with me into their adulthood and throughout their lives, I will be greatly satisfied. I have no interest in being their buddy or pal—I am content to be their father. But as the active, day-to-day rearing of Sam fades, if our relationship is to evolve—survive, even—that void must be filled with something else, with two adults forming a singular, unique relationship.

Having no template with my own father that I might follow, and since my first Camino proved so instrumental in my own maturation, I view this trip as an opportunity to actively begin Sam and my emotional transition.

At the breakfast table beside the modest buffet spread, Sam is staring down, apparently deep in thought. I wonder if he's considering his own version of these same weighty issues. Is he hoping this walk deepens our bond as well? Perhaps he's gathering himself for the long haul ahead. Maybe he's visualizing the walk, like a pro athlete might visualize a game he's about to enter.

Then he hisses, "Look."

"What?"

"Look where I'm pointing." There is very real strain in his voice. "There's a black hair on my prosciutto."

The look on Sam's face is so pained, so stricken, that for an instant it feels as if this errant lock has the power to derail our entire journey. I back away from joining him in taking this horror personally. A parent can orchestrate only so much of his child's experience. Eventually everyone must navigate the stray hairs of life on their own—and this seems like as good a moment as any to start establishing that adult-to-adult relationship.

"Grab something else, you're going to get hungry."

"I just want to get going." He pushes his chair back.

Out on the street, we head to the nearby Accueil des Pèlerins (Pilgrims' Office). Because we are getting such a late start, the office is empty, save for the lone, smiling volunteer who speaks a Spanish that sounds distinctly like French. I understand little he says, but we acquire our Pilgrim passports—papers that fold like an accordion and must be stamped at each stop along the way as proof of our journey when we reach Santiago. The volunteer also suggests we each take one of the scallop shells off the table behind us—the traditional pilgrim symbol that nearly all walkers carry, often affixing them to the outside of their backpack. A badge of pride.

I have a surprise for Sam, one I've brought from home, something it took me days of obsessive searching to find. And I've imagined a touching scene as we are about to set out.

"I have something I want to give you," I'd say to my son.

"What is it, Dad?" he'd reply.

I would then unwrap my carefully folded handkerchief containing an old scallop shell.

"I don't understand," he might say, a crease in his brow.

"I carried this across Spain on my first Camino, before you were born. I've kept it all these years. Would you like to carry it?"

"Oh, Dad," my son would exclaim and throw his arms around me.

But before any of this can happen, Sam turns to the table. "This one's fine," he says, and grabs a shell.

My sentimental fantasy fizzles. I say nothing. It is, after all, his Camino, I tell myself. I select a new shell as well and decide to leave my old one buried deep in my pack, unmentioned. In truth, I had mixed feelings about burdening my son with lugging around a relic of my past—the sins-of-the-father are enough without such obvious metaphors.

Our next stop is one of the many shops that have sprung up since my last trip, when pilgrim services were scant. Over the ensuing decades, an entire industry has evolved to aid those walking to Santiago—and in turn, the locals. We each choose a long walking stick and are finally ready to go.

"I gotta go poop," Sam says.

I actually slap my forehead.

Back in the room we make final preparations. I rearrange the weight in my backpack one last time. I urge Sam to get off his phone and get ready.

"Chill, bro. It's my last five minutes on TikTok."

Then he's trying on his new hat in front of the mirror. My son looks so young, his features so soft, his blue eyes sparkling. His wide and crooked grin matches my own. We're both giddy and nervous with excitement. I grab a few rushed photos of Sam as he hoists his pack. The shots are blurry because neither of us can stop moving. Despite my poor photographic efforts, the images reveal a young man so innocent, so excited and open and vulnerable—none of Sam's usual cool demeanor is present in this moment. And we're out the door.

"I'm tired"

484 miles to Santiago

Having walked for less than a hundred yards, Sam stops to tie his shoe on the cobblestone bridge over the River Nive.

"I'm tired," he says.

This comment elicits in me both panic and frustration in equal measure.

"Well, what would you like to do, Sam?"

"Nothing, I'm just saying."

Tension, born over the anxiety of beginning, flares between us. I redirect and take out my phone to snap a selfie of us. I take several.

"You're not going to keep doing that, are you?"

Since we're off to such a shaky start, I decide to compound the problem by giving my son some Camino history.

In the year 813 AD, in the far western reach of Spain, a hermit named Pelayo followed a ray of light that led him to a cave. There, he discovered the long-forgotten remains of the Apostle James.

"Oh my God. Seriously?" Sam groans and pushes off the wall and starts over the bridge.

The Bible offers little detail of James other than upon receiving the call, he immediately left his father's side while casting fishing nets to follow Jesus. James had the good fortune to be in the right place at the right time and witness some of early Christianity's greatest hits, such as the Transfiguration and Christ weeping in the Garden of Gethsemane. He also had the hubris to request to be seated at the right side of Jesus in heaven. The Lord was having none of that.

"Please stop," Sam says.

Legend goes on to tell us that after Christ's crucifixion, resurrection, and ascension, James headed off to the Iberian Peninsula in order to preach the Word. But he seemed to lack persuasiveness, or at least the oratory skills required to hold a crowd. He attracted just seven disciples for his troubles. Fortunately, the Virgin Mary appeared to James on the banks of the Ebro River. This apparition convinced him to return to Judea, where he was soon martyred by King Herod Agrippa's sword in the year 44, thus ensuring his legacy.

"And the story gets better," I promise Sam.

"I hope so," he says. We lean into the increasing grade.

"Angels then carried his body—and decapitated head—and placed it in a stone boat. They guided it safely across the sea and back to Spain. And it's a good thing they did, since the boat had no rudder, oar, or sail. On arrival, a few of James's remaining disciples took the body and buried it in a nearby cave, where it remained undisturbed and forgotten for eight hundred years—until Pelayo came along. Remember Pelayo, the hermit?"

"Sure," Sam lies. I don't think he's listening at all anymore.

The hermit/shepherd notified the local priest of his discovery. The bishop authenticated the relics. King Alfonso II built a chapel, and the devout came running, or rather, walking. By the eleventh century, a thousand pilgrims a day were reaching Santiago, inspired by the plenary indulgences promising the complete remission of temporal punishment for successful completion of the pilgrimage. In short, a lot of time in purgatory could be spared by a good long walk.

A cynic might argue that the discovery of James's remains, and the Church's consecration of this remote spot, had political motivations. Islamic Moors had taken over the majority of the Iberian Peninsula by this time in the ninth century, and the Church wanted it back. It proclaimed, in essence, "While you're walking across Spain to purify your almighty soul, slaughter those damn Moors." And when it was announced that Saint James had appeared atop a mighty steed and helped to slay the advancing Muslim hoards, the deal was sealed. The faithful couldn't be stopped.

By the Renaissance, with Spain now firmly in the hands of the Catholic Church, the Camino no longer held such sway and fell out of favor. The trail languished for several centuries, with few making the walk. It wasn't until the second half of the twentieth century, thanks to the efforts of a few local priests and later the Spanish tourism office, that interest in the pilgrimage was revived and began to grow again.

"So, he's buried in the cathedral?" Sam surprises me by demonstrating that he was, at least partially, listening.

"Well, maybe."

The Catholic Church has backed away from their stance that the remains of Saint James are in fact in Santiago, or that James was ever in Spain at all, for that matter. The word "tomb" is no longer mentioned in reference to the Cathedral as the place of James's final resting. Nor is the word "relic" to be spoken in reference to what may or may not be buried below the High Altar. Pope Benedict XVI walked things back even further when he said that the Cathedral is merely "linked to the memory of Saint James."

But the ever-increasing number of pilgrims marching across the north of Spain seem undeterred by all this political posturing, and such trivialities are certainly of no interest to Sam.

"Dad." He stops my discourse.

"I know, Sam, I know. I just thought it's interesting."

My son is gracious enough, or bored enough, to remain silent.

Leaving town behind on the Rue d'Espagne, we begin the climb up into the mountains. Saint-Jean has only 1,500 residents, but it takes some time to leave the red-tiled roofs of society behind. Low clouds cool the air. Cornfields supplant houses. A pair of pilgrims ahead of us, struggling with their packs, offer sheepish grins as we pass.

"It's weird, isn't it, Sammy?"

"What is?"

"This. We're just walking. That's the whole thing. The whole trip. There's nothing more complicated than this, across the whole country."

"Yeah, and?"

"The rest of it, it's all in your head."

"Everything is, Dad."

"I can't articulate what I mean."

"Well," my son advises me, "you have a whole country to figure it out."

Farther on, an older woman with a smooth gait moves at a steady pace.

"She's got a good, strong stride, doesn't she?" I say, and realize I sound like my father. My dad would often comment on those we passed on the street, or in the car. Most unsettling for me as a young boy were the times he remarked on the attractiveness of women. "She's a cutie," was a favorite line I always found unsettling.

"I think she's just having a walk," Sam says, and the woman, without a pack, turns up the path to her home.

"Ah," I mumble. Then recovering, I spot something ahead. "Look," I say, nodding to an oak tree by the side of the road. A large yellow arrow, pointing in the direction we are walking, has been painted on the bark. "We follow those all the way to Santiago."

"Seriously?" Sam asks. "I thought you were joking when you said that."

"Nope. Just keep your eye out."

It takes scant navigational skill to walk these five hundred miles; all that's required is to follow the arrows across the entire country.

A little farther on, Sam calls out like he's spotted Moby Dick's spout.

"There's one!" He's pointing to an arrow painted on a rock. Then there's another, down on the pavement. And another.

For several miles, we climb a steep, winding grade over narrow tarmac. Fog hangs low, snaking through the valley below. Sheep graze in a field. Three donkeys bray as we pass. Dense spider webs, shimmering with moisture, engulf clusters of heather. Everything appears lush and swollen, the height of summer. We come upon several groups of pilgrims, some laboring. With a rhythm of walking and habit-life on the road not yet established, the excitement and adrenaline of the first day is in many ways negated by the anxiety over the unknown. At more than fifteen miles, with an elevation gain of greater than four thousand feet, the first day on the road to Santiago is among the most arduous of the journey.

By late morning, Sam strips his sweatshirt off without stopping, moving his pack to one shoulder, twisting, shrugging, tugging, then shifting his load and repeating the process on the other side.

"God, I smell worse than I ever have in my life," he says.

"Thanks for sharing, Sam."

We come upon a stone building with picnic tables out front, positioned to look out over the deep ravine. As we've gained significant elevation, the view must be expansive, but we've no way of knowing, since dense fog has settled into the valley below. A dozen walkers mill about, resting, eating, drinking. Inside, I ask for my first café con leche since the last time I walked across Spain. Not a coffee drinker back home, the café con leche has some kind of hold over me—a caffeinated milkshake for adults. When I place the frothy brew down on the table, Sam looks up from his Coke.

"You don't drink coffee, Dad."

"Try it."

Sam shakes his head. "I don't like coffee."

"Just take a sip."

He does. "Yo, bro, will you order me one of those?"

"Café con leche," I say. "It couldn't be easier," encouraging him to practice some Spanish.

"Oh, come on."

"Teach a man to fish, Sammy. . . ."

"Spare me."

I shrug.

"Never mind," he says.

I get up and go to the bar—this adult-to-adult thing is going to take some practice.

"I don't know if I'm gonna get anything out of doing this"

475 miles to Santiago

Hours later, we're walking over tundra, high in rolling mountains. A stout man in a black beret stands among a heard of black-faced sheep, prized for their milk, used in Basque cheeses. Clouds stitch themselves into the valleys below. The fog has burned off, only to roll in again, obliterating our view, chilling the air, then dissipating just as quickly, leaving the sun burning down, the vistas long once more. Purple, yellow, magenta wildflowers bloom from the gorse. We pause in a field to eat a sandwich, then hear a metallic clanging growing louder. Three horses with bells around their necks trot over the hill and come to stand beside us, just a few feet away. Then two more join. We're all silent, looking out together. No one moves. Then the fog returns. The lead horse turns his head toward us; does he nod? He begins to trot slowly off. The others follow and disappear into the mist, the clang of their receding bells the only record of our encounter. Sam turns to me.

"Cool," he whispers.

My legs have begun to stiffen. I need to move. We pass an old, abandoned, and windowless, cinder block structure—slightly bigger than a shed. I poke my head inside. There are benches, a simple fireplace, some graffiti. It's a primitive and seldom used pilgrim's shelter—a port for a storm, and one that hints at a harsher journey than I hope to have. Yet I'm aware of a part of me that would like to stay here, or rather, would like to need to stay here. The satisfaction of needs asserting themselves and being met simply, superseding daily luxuries due to the severity of circumstances, is something in which I have found deep value on the few instances that it's been demanded in my life. And it's something I'd like my son to experience. But seeking out hardship is the dubious indulgence of a pampered fool. We march on without comment.

At one point Sam sees me taking notes on a small pad.

"Did you take notes last time?"

A friend had given me a small diary before I left on that first trip, suggesting I might write down thoughts or feelings that emerged along the way. I found the writing made me uncomfortable, forcing me to knock on a door I didn't care to open. A few hundred miles down the trail the Camino would kick that door open, but so early on that added introspection on top of what the walking already provoked was more than I could bear.

"I gave up after a few days," I confess to Sam.

"Exactly. I mean, fucking why?"

The border with Spain is marked by an obelisk with a scallop shell carved into it. Sam and I rap it with our walking sticks as we cross over a cattle grate and into another country. There are no guards, no fences. The dirt footpath, the topography, the sunshine, it's all the same. Our spirits rise.

"I don't know if I'm gonna get anything out of doing this walk," Sam says. "I'd like to have a profound experience, but I don't know if I will."

I must have been looking for a similarly transformative experience when I decided to come here on my first trek, but at this point in the journey, I lacked the courage to admit it to myself. I was focused solely on keeping my anxiety at bay and not getting lost and dying in the Pyrenees.

A shadow passes over my son—literally, from above. I look up into the now cloudless sky. A mature griffon vulture—whose wingspan can grow to eight feet—rides an air current overhead, scanning for carrion.

I want to assure Sam that the walk will be worth his time, that yes, great insights will come to him; life-changing thoughts that will benefit him are footsteps away. Over the years, I have made such pronouncements to my children when I perceived self-doubt or heard fear in their voices ("Of course Santa is real!"). But such assurances would be infantilizing to Sam now. My son is man enough to realize that I can't know. My baseless assertions, no matter how well intentioned, would only succeed in making him value my opinions less. And who am I really looking to assuage with them?

Just past an elevation of 4,688 feet (we started at 557), the end to our first day's trek comes into view. In the valley below, only a few miles off, are the rooftops of the abbey at Roncesvalles.

Starting down, I feel the instant strain on my knees. I also feel the weight of the journey ahead—somehow plunging into the valley commits us in a way that the long climb up did not. Paradoxically, I experience a very real sense of relief upon knowing we will make our day's goal. Such relief is something I would feel walking with anyone I had brought here. But this is my son who's joined me on this lark. And although I no longer bear the burden in a legal sense, responsibility for his physical safety is something I feel more acutely here than in day-to-day life, when routine and familiarity pacify those fears into a more padded corner of the mind.

My knee twinges, and it occurs to me that there are only a handful of people with whom I am close and wouldn't feel such a sense of responsibility. Over the years, these have tended to be slightly older men, often physically larger than me, and in whose presence I experience the relief of burden and sensation of safety that I am usually unaware I lack. A psychologist might easily explain this away—my older brother Peter was my protector as a child. In his care, I felt watched over, seen, and liked in a way that I never did with my father. No one dared mess with me at school on Peter's watch.

The rolling Navarre landscape spreads out below, and Sam begins to wonder aloud about the root of jealousy, its corroding potency.

"It's a real problem. It's like I can't stop thinking about it."

It is Sam's first mention of his life with The Ex.

"They don't call it the green-eyed monster for nothing," I say.

"Do you get jealous?"

"I never told you about Dolores and my honeymoon?"

On safari with Sam's stepmom in Mozambique, I grew suspicious of our guide's attention to my new wife ("Dolores, come sit up here beside me; you can see better"). I became more closed in, more remote, silently creating scenarios in my mind until my wife confronted me on my suddenly distant mood. When I confessed my jealousy, she laughed, then picked up the book I was reading, Hemingway's *The Snows of Kilimanjaro,* in which the wife of the dying narrator is having an affair with their safari guide.

"Don't you think you could have been a bit more creative?" she asked.

My jealousy burst, and we laughed.

"But I still resent that fucker," I assure Sam. "The point is that jealousy can make you insane. It clouds your ability to see a situation clearly."

"I guess."

My pack jostles against my back with each descending step. I cinch it tighter.

"Did you ever regret getting divorced from Mom?" Sam asks, seemingly from nowhere.

Carol and I divorced when Sam was two. And it's clear that everything will be on the table during this walk.

"Oh, Sammy," I say. "It's complicated. Regret's not the right word. It was sad, for sure. It took me a long time to realize I had to mourn the loss of the relationship, even though I was the one who ended things."

While he was still a very young child, I mentioned to a friend that Sam and I had a frank conversation about why his parents split up. My friend listened and said, "It's a conversation you will have again and again." Her observation was both astute and prescient. During each phase of Sam's maturity, the topic has circled back, each time going a little deeper, closer to the core. Each time, I've had to take a deep breath and commit to honoring his need to know. And now that Sam has joined the adult ranks of someone having a former romantic partner, his view on the subject has gained an added, perhaps more nuanced, perspective.

"I do believe that everyone's better off now than we would have been had Mom and I stayed married," I say.

"I know," Sam says.

We walk in silence for a few knee-jarring steps. "I guess at the end of the day, Sam, I felt like I had to leave fifteen percent of myself at the door. Which is entirely an indictment of me and not in any way a reflection on your mother. Maybe it was just my selfishness."

The safe haven of Roncesvalles is ahead now. We're silent again. Our footfalls are the only sound.

"Dad," Sam says at last, "is anyone trustworthy?"

I swallow hard.

The first pilgrim refuge at Roncesvalles was built in 1127 and promised "the door opens to all, the sick and healthy, not only true Catholics, but also pagans, Jews, heretics, the idle and vagabonds." Sam and I must fit somewhere on that list; I push open the heavy wooden door.

When I arrived in Roncesvalles a quarter century earlier, there were eight other walkers sheltering in one vast, dark, dank room with more than a hundred bunks. This new, multifloored, clean and bright facility divided into discrete cubicles sleeps nearly double that number and is my first real indication just how much the Camino has matured since my last visit.

There will be similar, if smaller, pilgrim albergues at each town along the way. They are the primary support for housing weary pilgrims. Initially run exclusively by, and often located adjacent to, the local church, as the Camino gained in popularity, independent hostels sprang up as well. Most are spartan, with dormitory rooms and bunk beds; others are almost lavish in their accommodations.

Inside, a rake-thin man is eager to welcome us and stamp our pilgrim credentials. When I marvel at the state of the new facility, he proudly asks if we'd like a bed.

"We have less than half the usual walkers," he tells us. "Come," and he spreads his arms, indicating that we follow.

But my memory of sagging mattresses on rusting beds and dubious communal showers led me to reserve a room at the converted monastery next door. When I inform our would-be host, he reacts as if slapped; his eyes blink in rapid succession. He invites us to leave. Now.

On my last Camino, I slept in pilgrim albergues roughly half the walk, opting at other times for small inns. I experienced occasional jabs from fellow walkers about this. At one communal dinner, a Dutch walker snapped, "But you are not a real pilgrim; you stay in hotels with showers."

I turned to him. "Isn't the Camino helping you discard that judgment of others?"

The Dutchman glared at me.

"Just walk your own Camino, Hans," the German woman beside him scolded.

Hans buried his eyes in his beans.

I was a credit-card pilgrim and made no apologies. Twenty-six years later, the thought of having people stepping on me to get to their top bunk and waiting for the toilet appeals to me even less. Sam and I turn on our heels, walk across the courtyard, and enter the converted monastery.

After the perpetual motion of the day, Sam finds it difficult to settle in our clean, spartan room. Because Roncesvalles has such a storied and bloody history, dating back to the death of Roland in 778 AD, when he was slaughtered by local Basques while leading Charlemagne's retreating army and was later made famous as the hero of medieval poetry and song—I'm tempted to think the place might be of some interest to Sam. I'm wrong. With a permanent population of just thirty, and neither the cloisters, a church, nor a museum of any interest to my son, he is quickly bored.

"What are we supposed to do now?" Sam asks.

I can offer no help. Lying on my back atop the bed, my legs are inverted, with my feet high up on the wall above the headboard—they are visibly throbbing. My hands and fingers have begun to tingle. The rest of my body is numb. My phone tells me I have walked 40,527 steps and climbed the equivalent of 422 flights of stairs.

"Go get a Coke."

Sam moves about like a caged animal. "That was a long fucking walk."

I continue to stare at the ceiling. I'm finding it difficult to speak.

"What's the point?"

468 miles to Santiago

I got a call from Sam the day before we left for Spain.

"Dad?"

I knew that tone.

"Yes, Sam."

"Can you do me a favor?"

"I hope so."

"And not get mad?"

"Go on."

"Can you get me some Nicorette gum for the trip?"

Pause.

"Um . . . why can't you get it?"

"You have to be twenty-one."

I thought about what to say next. "You realize you're an absolute idiot."

"Yeah, I know."

Apparently, a few months earlier, Sam had begun occasionally and in secret to smoke cigarettes. They had "snuck up on him." He had gnawed a few pieces of the gum back in Saint-Jean and during our first day on the trail. This morning, that novelty has worn off. "But don't worry, Dad. I'll have long quit by the time we get even halfway there."

It's after 9:00 a.m. Every other walker is long gone. We're standing out front of the monastery, getting ready to go. Fog and drizzle make the cool air sharp. Sam points to a couple, tourists, standing by a bench. The man is smoking.

"Can you go ask that guy for a cigarette?"

"Not a chance."

"But you speak Spanish."

"No, I don't."

"You actually do. I'm really surprised how well you can speak it. Where'd you learn all that?"

I glare at my son. "I raised you to manipulate better than that. If you want one, go ask yourself."

I spend the next five minutes teaching Sam how to ask for a cigarette in the local language.

Roncesvalles, our single-minded goal only yesterday, is left quickly behind. The trail skirts the road, where a sign announces a distance of 790 kilometers to Santiago de Compostela, then plunges under mature beech and oak trees that the light rain can't penetrate. Moss-covered stone walls flank the path. We duck under gnarled branches.

I attempt a bit more history. "This area is called the Oak Grove of Witches. Secret covens were convened here in the sixteenth century."

Sam doesn't bite.

"It's interesting though, isn't it?" I press on. "Kind of brings the landscape to life a bit?"

"I guess." Sam managed to butcher enough Spanish to squeeze two cigarettes out of the defenseless tourist. He fires the first one up and sticks the other behind his ear. "I'll save it till the end of the day. Where are we going?"

"Zubiri."

"Is there more going on there than this place?"

"Some. It's a small industrial town. I remember it not being that nice."

"How far?"

I consult my book. "Thirteen and a half miles."

"You really need to look at your book? Haven't you looked like a hundred times already today?"

I have not one but two small guidebooks—listing distances, accommodations, points of interest, etc. I consult them constantly, and just as quickly forget everything I've read. Add to this that in the life of a walker, pertinent information on any given locale becomes instantly obsolete the moment we pass.

"When do we get somewhere good?"

By good, I know Sam means a place with some action, or at least a gym where he can work out.

"This is all about the journey, Sammy."

"Oh my God, did you actually just say that?"

"I know, but it's true. It's not that the places we get to aren't cool; some of them are great, like Pamplona tomorrow. It's a great city." We pass a white cross, originally erected to "purify" the magic of the local witches.

Concluding that there really is no point in waiting, Sam lights his other cigarette.

Emerging from the trees an hour later, we come upon a small village. Water races through deep gutters. Geraniums fill window boxes. Hemingway wrote of the "red roofs and white houses of Burguete" in *The Sun Also Rises*. In the stark town square, there is no evidence of the nine women who were burned at the stake here during the Inquisition. Continuing out of town, as we cross over a small footbridge and head into open fields, Sam informs me that Shakespeare was bisexual.

"Really?"

"They have love letters he wrote to men."

There are scores of books written about how parents might best educate and raise their children, but one of the more pleasurable and underreported aspects of parenting are the things kids teach their parents. That said, I have no idea if there's any truth in Sam's statement.

Considering the ramifications of his remark, I miss the transition my son makes to the cruel, even abusive behavior of mixed martial arts fighter Conor McGregor—or, as is more likely, maybe there was no transition at all, except inside his head. When I claim no knowledge of McGregor, Sam stops in his tracks.

"What rock are you living under?"

"Hey," I shoot back, "do you know who Mike Tyson is?"

"Of course I know who Mike Tyson is. What's the matter with you?"

"Well, I'm just saying."

"What are you just saying?"

"I'm just saying that, like . . ." I run out of steam. "OK, fine."

We walk on. Sam is silent for a moment, then explores the topic of the casual cruelty we'd been discussing through a more personal lens.

"That's one thing that she taught me."

I know, of course, that Sam is referring to The Ex. "What is?"

"That it's cool to be kind. I had this stupid idea that just dissing people was cool."

I nod, grateful Sam has arrived at this conclusion, no matter at whose urging. I've had mixed feelings about certain aspects of Sam's relationship with his now former girlfriend, but there is of course no arguing with her stance on this topic.

The conversation widens out to a more conceptual discussion of rage, and its perils. Then it zooms in again. This time, on my impetus.

"I experienced rage with my father, Sam. It's no fun."

Sam met my father on exactly two occasions. The first time I had taken him, his sister, Willow, and my wife, Dolores, up to Maine, where my dad lived with his second wife, Ursula.

It had not been my idea. "They've never met their grandfather," Dolores insisted to me on multiple occasions. "We need to go." So, finally, we did.

My father and his wife welcomed us sweetly. I wandered through the house, disoriented to see a coffee table and a single painting of a sea-scape that had been in my childhood home. Nothing else of our shared life remained. After dinner, my father suggested ice cream. He insisted I drive us all in his old Chevy with one working headlight through a torrential rain to the Ice Cream Barn. He ordered one scoop each of chocolate and vanilla and spent a long time mixing the two flavors until they were one. As I drove his car back, squinting into the darkness, wind-shield wipers slapping hard, he sat beside me and ate. I had never seen someone savor ice cream more.

"How did I not know my dad loved ice cream?" I asked Dolores that night as I slipped into bed in the guestroom of my father's home.

"What are you doing?" Dolores asked me.

I was still wearing my underwear. Dolores had never seen me sleep anything but naked.

"I don't know." I shrugged. "I just feel funny."

When her laughter subsided, she asked with tenderness, "You don't feel safe in your dad's house?"

I shrugged. "I never did."

On the other occasion, I had invited my father down to New York to meet Rowan, our newborn. My father's condition had continued the deterioration I'd first noticed several years earlier in Maine. Dementia had begun to assert itself. He and Ursula arrived, and he doted on his new grandson. The following evening, he became confused going down a flight of stairs instead of up. When Willow, then seven, tried to help him, my father exploded in rage familiar from my youth. My reaction was swift and severe. They left my home the following morning, a day early.

"He got angry a lot, huh?" Sam asks as we pass two horses standing motionless in a field.

"A lot? I don't know, what's a lot? But when he did, it was volcanic. In hindsight, it seems a lot. It's what stands out, unfortunately."

But now, suddenly, Sam and I are talking high fashion. My son's interest is far greater than mine, and already—according to me—he spends too much on clothes.

"They say a lot, Dad."

"I know, you're right. I just don't really care."

"Well, that's..." My son shakes his head.

And now we're into a spirited discussion on the wokeness of our current culture. I miss a point Sam is making on gender vs. sex.

"Don't just be a dinosaur willfully, Dad."

It's the kind of freewheeling talk, some of it meaningful, some trivial, that walking inspires. We ford another small stream over stepping-stones, and Sam turns the talk to my career. I'm made instantly uncomfortable by the topic.

"Your legacy doesn't have to be just what you did when you were a kid," Sam says. "There's still time."

As a young man, I had achieved a certain type of fame, appearing as an actor in the youth films of the day that I helped to popularize. My success proved a double-edged sword. Those movies defined my place in the world, and in myself, for decades—even as I moved on to other roles and other types of work, including television directing.

"You need to stop directing other people's shows, Dad," Sam goes on. "You're selling yourself short. You gotta do your own show or direct a movie." The frankness of his observation is only mildly difficult to hear.

The trail dumps us out onto a narrow road surrounded by beech trees.

"It takes a long time, if ever, to perceive your parents as normal people," Sam concludes.

Winding up and then down, we enter into a rhythmic stride and make strong progress. On the end of the long walking sticks we bought back in Saint-Jean, a pointed metal tip is attached. It creates a thin, metallic rap with each step. I begin to fixate on this sound.

"If we ever see somebody with a saw, I'm going to ask them if they'll trim the tip of my stick," I say to Sam. "I hate this metal sound."

We walk a dozen more strides, both now focusing on the harsh rapping.

"Now I can't hear anything else," Sam says. "Thanks a lot."

"Sorry, Sammy. But if we pass a hardware store, I'm getting a small handsaw."

Fifteen minutes later, we emerge from the beech forest. On the outskirts of the village, a man and woman are bent over a humming buzz saw, surrounded by piles of wood.

"No way." Sam laughs.

I smile. "Welcome to the Camino, my boy." Stories of such serendipity are legion along The Way.

I approach the man and ask if he can help us. He frowns at me for interrupting his work. Then leading me to the back of his nearby truck, he extracts a chain saw. I secure my stick as he trims off the offensive tip in seconds. Then he does the same for Sam. I offer to pay him, but he shakes off my gesture. He is all smiles as he waves goodbye. "*Buen Camino!*" he calls. His wife intones the same salutation, and Sam and I march on.

"*Buen Camino*" is an expression that is new since my last walk. It is well intentioned and supportive, spoken in solidarity, and has become ubiquitous along the road. It also strikes me as the kind of banal phrase that might have been the work of the Spanish tourist bureau.

We pass through the village and then in and out of more beechwood groves and open fields. Up and down gentle hills. A golden eagle glides overhead. The sun burns now. The day wears on.

Entering a forest of maple and wild cherry trees, the trail dives steeply down for the last few miles of the day. I'm not a nostalgic person by nature, but I've wondered how much I would find myself comparing this walk to my last. Before we began, I promised myself not to bore my son with stories of "Oh, last time...!" But as my foot slips out from under me and I almost go down on the steep grade, I'm reminded of when I passed through these woods long ago.

I was at a very different place in life. In my early thirties, single and childless, I was several years removed from a drinking habit that had derailed my life. I had put down cigarettes just eight months earlier. My movie career, which had once showed such promise, was essentially over. And I was terrified to be making this walk alone.

I had read about it in a book I picked up at random. Never having heard of the Camino de Santiago, and with no Internet to search, I tracked down the author of the book. I called him on the phone. Startled to receive such a call, Jack Hitt was gracious and generous when I told him I had read *Off the Road,* and I pounded him with questions about the walk. A week later, I was on a plane to Spain. What I hadn't counted on was the level of anxiety I would need to overcome. I muscled through that first day to Roncesvalles alone, but on this second day of the walk I attached myself to a young Spaniard who dressed in the costume of an old-time pilgrim, wearing a brown cloak and dark hat. He carried a long, hooked walking stick with a gourd affixed to the top. He looked like an overgrown trick-or-treater out of season. He spoke no English, and I had no Spanish. And unfortunately for him, we just happened to be setting out from Roncesvalles at the same instant. But six or seven hours into the day's walk, he had had enough of me. As he stopped in this same forest to tie the lace of his boot, he waved me on.

I indicated that I would wait.

Go on, he gestured again with his stick, this time more forcefully.

"I don't mind waiting, really," I assured him.

"GO!" he finally blurted in English.

Marching a few steps ahead of me now, Sam lays his walking stick across his shoulders and drapes his arms out along it. He has had enough for one day.

"Dad?" he calls over his shoulder.

"Yeah."

"I don't know if I'm gonna learn anything doing this bullshit."

I'm tired. I have little to offer him right now.

"Maybe not," I say.

"I mean, bro, what's the point of this fucking walk?"

"Is there an airport in Pamplona?"

454 miles to Santiago

I sleep poorly and wake in the middle of the night. No good comes from any conclusions drawn at 4:00 a.m. I know this but am unable to quiet my mind. I fear that I need more sleep for the day ahead or I may not be able to make it to Pamplona.

And I fear that my son may decide to quit. The reality of the walk is by now beginning to supersede any fantasies that may have been in his mind—fantasies no doubt implanted by my years of talking about the wonders of the Camino. My hope is that the rewards I know it possesses begin to emerge for Sam before fatigue or boredom or restlessness take hold.

For much of Sam's early life, I harbored the not-so-secret fear that my son would one day wake up and hate me. This sensitivity fueled over-attentiveness, favoritism, and any number of compensations that might in fact do much to ensure the end I'd hoped to avoid. The knowledge that my strained relationship with my own father was the clear seed for this anxiety offered just enough comfort to allow me to challenge its veracity. Sitting now on the side of the bed, I assure myself that the relationship I have with my son is not the relationship I had with my father—nor are we condemned to re-create it. The black of night calls me a liar.

My mind continues to grind in the dark. We should be sleeping in the albergue instead of this pleasant little inn, so Sam has a full Camino experience. So his world can expand. So he is not too pampered. So he is not stuck with only me for company. I am failing him. I am always on the edge of failing him—of failing all my children. My thoughts turn darker. I am failing my wife. She sounds happier on the phone with me gone. My thinking grows darker still, and it's clear to me that I don't know something, see something, understand something, that is essential to love. Maybe it's better for all if I'm alone.

Outside the window—right outside the window—a rooster begins to crow.

I open the shutter; the sky has begun to soften through a deep purple. The mattress sags under me as the vegetable garden emerges. Then the small, enclosed field beyond it. A few sheep sleep on the ground. On a not-so-distant hill, a cellphone tower rises. The rooster continues his morning chore.

Our inn is located on the banks of the Arga River at the foot of the arched, stone Puente de la Rabia. It was long believed that if a farmer marched his animals back and forth over the bridge three times, the beasts would be free of rabies. Maybe a similar recrossing might free my mind.

The town of Zubiri strings itself along a busy truck artery. The place lacks charm but contains just enough life to engage Sam. After I collapsed on the bed, my legs inverted and feet up the wall, he stalked the streets, talking to his friends back home on the phone. Then on the edge of town, at what turned out to be little more than a truck stop, we ate trout with serrano ham, a local delicacy. I have a singular memory of eating Trucha a la Navarra on my first Camino and it being the best meal I had in Spain. Not so this time. Full of bones and fatty ham, I left half of it on the plate, as did Sam—we went to get pizza and ice cream.

Then came the dark night and the rooster—which now gives no indication of stopping.

I let Sam sleep and head out for breakfast. When I return, he speaks before I have the door half open.

"That fucking rooster woke me up, bro."

"Good. We need to get going."

"If I had a gun, I'd shoot that fucking thing."

Teenagers are notoriously late risers, and Sam is no exception. The trouble is only partly in getting my son up. It is what happens after that causes me more distress. First, there is the bathroom. Whatever happens in there takes what it takes. And it takes a while. Then there is the repacking of the rucksack. On arrival each day, the contents of Sam's pack explode all over the room. Despite my repeated suggestion that he repack the night before so he is ready, each morning the process is begun from scratch.

Sam's apparent lack of interest in the task, the loss of focus once begun, the flat-out forgetting what he's doing, the TikTok that must be viewed at this exact instant, the window that must be stared out of— witnessing the process brings out the worst in me: impatience, controlling intolerance, frustration, wholesale panic for his future.

In Roncesvalles, I decided to leave him to pack and meet up outside. This proved to be a tactical error on my part. Sam never appeared. I had to go back up and get him. The solution I have arrived at today is to stand over my son and treat him like a child. ("Put your sunscreen on top; don't forget those socks on the radiator...") There is no obvious pleasure in this—although there is an unflattering facet of me that silently claims satisfaction in a dubious righteousness—and it is certainly not in service of my larger aim for this trip. I would never treat a peer like this. I justify my demeaning behavior by concluding that we need to get out the fucking door. But, to Sam's credit—and exacerbating my frustration—he appears largely oblivious to my agitation. This quality that my son possesses, whether true ignorance or a more innate wisdom of detachment, may be the single most important aspect that has, on more than one occasion, saved us from escalating into an ugly scene. This morning is no exception.

As I open the door, Sam asks me if I have an extra pad and pen. He might want to jot down a few things along the way.

"Sure," I say. Tossing him a pad, I congratulate myself on the maturity of my restraint in not mentioning his earlier dismissal of such an idea. My amusement at recognizing the childishness in my self-satisfaction doesn't make it any less juvenile. I need to start walking.

The moment we step onto the trail, my phone buzzes. My wife and daughter are on FaceTime. Whatever dire conclusions I came to a few hours ago in the dark are not substantiated by my family this morning. They appear delighted to talk with me. "Are you missing your favorite kid?" Willow asks. Full of questions about the trail so far, Dolores is an enthusiast whose passions are just as likely to be unreciprocated by me in a manner I know she desires and deserves. My inhibitions and easily aroused sense of shame do nothing to support her freewheeling vivacity. It's solely because of a love that often appears to us beyond our under-standing that my introversion and her extroversion do not implode us. But this morning, my two girls' delight in our venture is contagious. Their support spurs Sam and me on as we pass a magnesium factory that looms over Zubiri before joining a thin trail cutting through eye-high grass. Three vultures circle low in a thickening sky.

At the first small village, we barely break stride, but pass three pil-grims chatting, drinking water, and rearranging their packs.

"Is that an Irish accent?" I ask.

"From Cork," the red-faced man with an edgy manner snaps back. "You been?"

"I have," I tell him. The other two men are younger, from the States.

"New York," one says.

"We're from New York," Sam calls out. "Where?"

"Oyster Bay," the young man with a ready smile says.

"That's not New York," I tell him. "That's Long Island."

We all laugh. Sam and I keep walking. "Think we'll see them again?" Sam asks.

"The Camino is long, Sammy. I'd say we will."

The trail takes us down by the Arga River, and a low rumble of rolling thunder peels.

"Yo, bro, was that thunder?"

"I think so. Your poncho on top?"

"It's in there."

"Remember, I said to put it on top."

"Whatever, it's there." Sam has more philosophical things on his mind. "What are thoughts, anyway?"

"Um, what do you mean?"

"And recalling dreams is weird, because you're remembering something that didn't happen."

Before I can reply, a close crash of thunder gets my full attention. On cue, the rain pelts down. The air feels suddenly electric. My favorite word in Spanish is "tormentas," and we're in the midst of one now.

We stop by the side of the trail. I slip on my poncho; Sam digs for his. The river beside us roils.

Slogging on in silence, I trudge in Sam's footsteps.

Then my son calls over his shoulder, "Is there an airport in Pamplona?"

Reminded of my wife's advice that in dealing with kids (and adults), there's often little wrong that a nap or a snack won't fix, and since sleep is currently out of the question, I suggest food.

We drop our packs and sit by the side of the trail in the rain on a large, exposed root under dense canopy. I pull out my packet of serrano ham; Sam pulls out his salami. We eat wet meat.

A kingfisher flitters on the bank, ruffling its feathers in the rain. Rain drips from the hoods of our ponchos onto our faces and food. We begin to laugh.

After wiping our greasy hands on the wet grass, ten minutes later we cross the Arga River on the Puente de Zuriain. On the far bank is the rustic but welcoming Café la Parada, with a covered patio overlooking the river. Nearly two dozen pilgrims taking shelter from the storm are drinking coffee and chatting in small clusters. Faces have begun to look familiar. The three middle-aged Spanish ladies—one with pink, the other with purple, the third with green dyed hair—flash bright smiles as we arrive. There is the trim and overtly athletic-looking French couple. A half dozen boisterous Italians. We nod greetings. I chat with a Dutchman while ordering our café con leche. The Irishman and the two American lads make a ruckus as they join the impromptu gathering. Irish comes over to shake hands. Sam chats with Oyster Bay.

I snap a few candid photos. Sam takes my phone, scrolls through, and shakes his head. "Parents are incapable of not taking bad pictures of their children."

I take back the phone, find a few nice shots, and show him.

Sam is dismissive. "They all give off the flowering children vibe."

This is typical of the type of phrase Sam employs that I don't understand.

"You can't get the sense from what I'm saying? Come on, Dad, you're fairly smart—work it out."

I sip my café con leche.

As much as Sam wisely observed that it takes a long while, if ever, for children to see their parents as real people, perhaps the inverse is equally true.

The rain lets up. People begin to hoist their packs and walk on. Sam doesn't move. "These breaks in the middle of the walk are the best part of the day."

Once we're back on the trail, Sam pauses at an underpass below the N-135 to jot down some notes. He's been talking about The Ex, unpacking it, clarifying.

"Anger," he mutters, crouched and leaning against the graffiti-covered wall.

I nod.

"It's helpful to write this shit down," he says. "And the walking is good."

I'm aware that I am currently in possession of that greatest of parental luxuries with an adult child—time. And it allows me to maintain some remove and not feel the need to rush in with advice or fixes. Each person's first heartache is the first heartache ever and needs to be honored as such. Let the Camino do its work, I silently remind myself. Just walk along beside him.

By the time we enter Pamplona through the Portal de Francia, carved into the city's sixteenth-century walls of fortification, Sam has exhausted the topic of The Ex for the day and is expounding on the ferocity of black holes. "They terrify me," he says. When I fail to exhibit the proper awe at something so far beyond my comprehension, Sam attempts again to explain about energy and force and the finality they present. "It's insane," he concludes his tutorial.

"You think that's insane," I say, "try running through these narrow streets being chased by angry bulls."

Ernest Hemingway brought Pamplona's Fiesta de San Fermín to the attention of the world in his novel *The Sun Also Rises*. The swift, the drunk, and the macho from around the globe have been coming ever since. Attempting to outrun bulls let loose in the city each morning for a week in early July, the goal is to make it to the bullring without getting gored. Invariably, some don't.

The first time I was in Pamplona, I had to stop for three days to let my blisters heal—and while not a twenty-four-inch horn through the spleen, they did hurt a lot. I had purchased heavy leather hiking boots the day before my departure from New York. Everyone knows you need to break in heavy leather hiking boots. I apparently thought this didn't apply to me.

The anxiety I felt upon starting my Camino had not abated, and I was tempted to use my bleeding feet as an excuse to abort my walk and go home. But I had boasted to friends that I would be gone for a month while I walked across Spain. Fear of further humiliation dictated that I carry on. And there was another reason, a more troubling reason, I needed to continue. Not long before my journey it had dawned on me, at last, that I had great difficulty in finishing anything I started. It may have been the first shining of a light on an old habit that had existed for so long in the dark of my consciousness, but in my newfound awareness it seemed everything I did went unfinished. I couldn't even complete a newspaper article. A few sentences from the end, I would become distracted or lose interest. It felt as if only with the greatest of effort and deliberate, deep breathing could I complete even the simplest tasks.

Making it to Santiago altered that pattern. I became someone who saw things through.

Maybe I just project too much of my own emotional baggage onto my loved ones, but I fear a similar habit emerging in my son. He quit karate after years and just before getting his black belt—how many hours had I watched through the glass as he kicked and whirled? And Sam's schoolwork usually remained incomplete. "I'm basically finished" became a catchphrase in our home that filled me with dread. I want my son to get to Santiago. I want him to have that satisfaction of completion in his bones. My telling him—and all my children—to "finish strong" means nothing compared with wearing out a pair of shoes across the country.

As I lead Sam into the regal Plaza del Castillo, Pamplona's main square, we pass a round man in a black beret playing an accordion and eighteenth-century buildings with pedestrian arcades and wrought-iron balconies. I found Pamplona, a city of two hundred thousand, and the largest town along The Way, a welcoming place so many years ago. I've been looking forward to my return. I point out the belle epoque Café Iruña, Hemingway's favorite haunt. Sam is looking around, taking it all in, nodding. Europe has always been an eye-opening experience for a young American, and I'm aware that my son is seeing this for the first time. I'm excited for his reaction, his perspective, his insights, maybe even his gratitude to me for taking him here. Finally, he speaks.

"I wonder why they don't have Flamin' Hot Cheetos in Europe."

"Mal Camino"

441 miles to Santiago

I wake to snarling. A vicious-sounding dog outside is growling and barking, and then gets dragged away. I stretch my suddenly brittle body and head out for an early Sunday morning look around. The cobbled streets of Pamplona are deserted. Graffiti-covered gates securing shops are pulled down tight. Only the street cleaners are out. Powerful hoses attached to the back of slow-moving water trucks armed by men in yellow vests spray down the streets, washing away all traces of a summer Saturday night's revelries.

In an effort to avoid another hassle getting Sam out of bed, I suggested a ten o'clock start. We were up late in the swarming Pamplona streets. We attempted a tapas crawl, but my lack of foodie passion couldn't summon enough enthusiasm to carry the day eating things I not only couldn't pronounce but couldn't identify, while Sam, who is much more adventurous with food than I, felt naturally self-conscious during his first night in the bustling bars with a language he couldn't communicate in and combinations of food so alien to him. After a few anchovies over egg covering something mysterious, we grabbed pizza.

Beside wishing to avoid a fight, my suggestion to leave late had an ulterior motive—I want to spend some time at Café Iruña. I passed much of my three days in Pamplona there last time, chasing Hemingway's ghost, and recall it as the place I first relaxed while in Spain. I make my way to Plaza del Castillo. More street cleaners torment the pigeons trying to pick at the ground by the bandstand. The sun has yet to clear the buildings. There's a chill in the air.

Being happy is surpassed only by the ability to recognize and appreciate that happiness in the moment. The first customer at Café Iruña on this day, sitting at an outdoor table sipping a café con leche, eating a napolitana de chocolate, I'm giddy with contentment. In a foolish attempt to make a near perfect moment more nearly perfect, I order another coffee and another pastry. I regret my overindulgence—as I knew I would—and hustle back to rouse Sam. After the usual tussle, we're only an hour late hitting the road.

Walking out of a city is considerably more agreeable to the nervous system than walking into one. Emerging from the countryside onto paved roads, encountering trucks and traffic lights, buildings and commerce, and people, can be jarring. It seems unlikely that we could get used to the simplicity of society's absence after such a short time, but something in walking so intently demands attention to the present and explains why the days feel so full, even as little other than one foot after the other is taking place. And while the joys of the city are easily categorized, the excitement of setting out again outweighs the safety of the known.

The Camino leaving Pamplona is winding, and turns are readily missed. We miss several. Instead of yellow arrows pointing the way, there are small scallop-shell emblems embedded in the sidewalks—at times difficult to see amid all the urban distractions. If it weren't for the small old men in black berets whose sole purpose it seems is to sit on park benches and right errant pilgrims with the point of a cane, it would take us much longer than the hour it does to clear the city.

And then, all of a sudden, we're in the countryside again. The dirt trail is narrow and slices through fields of already cut wheat that will dominate much of our vista for the next month. We begin to climb foot-hills. A few hours' walk ahead, a dozen energy-generating windmills line the ridge of Alto del Perdón (Mount of Forgiveness). A pair of bikers squeezes past, forcing us off the narrow path and into a thicket. Then another pair.

One basic truth of the Camino is that walkers hate bikers. It will take those pedaling less than a week to complete the journey, but speed here is not the point, and we resent their air of superiority, their assumed sense of priority. Some try to be pleasant as they shove us aside, calling out *"Buen Camino!"* while coating us with dust.

"Mal Camino!" Sam shouts back.

"And what's with the costumes?" I ask Sam. "I've never understood this. Why do bikers the world over all play dress-up to go bike riding? They're not in the Tour de France. Aren't shorts and a T-shirt fine? Do they need to be aerodynamic in their spandex professional biker uni-forms? When I play basketball, I don't feel the need to put on a Knicks uniform." I'm getting up a head of steam now. "And whatever it is that they're doing here, they are not doing the Camino de Santiago. They bike for a few days, and they're done. They should just stay on the road, or better yet, stay home."

It's satisfying to vent about our biking cousins—a simple walker can feel pretty insignificant laboring over a vast and spinning globe.

After Pamplona, the topography shifts, and the walk begins to take on a scale that hadn't been apparent in the dramatic Pyrenees. The palette turns brown, while the vistas grow longer; the immensity of what's ahead is difficult to deny.

The path climbs steeply now, taking us through hawthorn and box-wood shrubs. The huge wind turbines above create an ominous hum. I search out La Fuente Reniega (Fount of Renunciation) close to the trail. Legend has it that, on this slope, the devil appeared to a tired and thirsty pilgrim three times in various guises, offering water if only the pilgrim would renounce first God, then the Virgin Mary, and finally Saint James. Each time the pilgrim refused. The devil finally vaporized in a cloud of sulfur, and James himself appeared, offering the devout pilgrim water from his scallop shell. It was on this spot that a deep and rich well of sweet water sprang up. Perhaps, but the earth here has long been parched by the time we huff past.

The ridge is dominated by a massive sheet-metal sculpture of pilgrims from various eras, walking the trail. It was erected the year after my last walk and has become emblematic of the Camino. A Swedish family, a husband and wife and their three blond children, are standing, taking in the view, their car by the side of the narrow ridge road. They look bored, listless.

When the father asks what we're doing, the gravity with which he nods his head upon hearing my reply allows me to acknowledge in a deeper way than I had up to now, that yes, this walk I am taking with my son is a big deal and is a worthwhile endeavor.

Sam appears to be feeling some sense of pride as well as we pose for a photo the Swedish man snaps. Or perhaps Sam is just puffing up for the teenage daughters, although when the girls hear what we're doing, they react as if we have volunteered for electric shock treatment.

Sam and I turn back for a last look at Pamplona in the valley behind us and the Pyrenees beyond. As we head into what is clearly new geography, it feels very much as if the introduction to the Camino is behind us. We turn into the afternoon sun, drop down off the ridge, and head west.

The decline is steep, very. I slip twice, my backpack throwing off my equilibrium when I lose balance. Even Sam slides badly. "Fuck the downhill," he shouts over his shoulder.

Slowing up, Sam holds out his hand, offering me one of his earbuds.

"This is Bo Burnham's show I was telling you about."

That it's easy for an older generation to dismiss the entertainment of those coming of age is not news. And I've been guilty of such laziness. There's something about the intensity of youth, coupled with its audacity, that exerts a power often dismissed by those who've grown older and forgotten their own reckless early days. Listening to Burnham, I'm reminded that I do so to my own detriment. Not only is Burnham a damn good distraction on the knee-pounding descent, but he and the other voices my children are listening to offer insight into what's important to them, as well as how they think and communicate. Burnham's almost Tourette-like candor, coupled with his humor, reveal a frankness that my children's generation appear comfortable inhabiting in a way mine never did.

My occasional resistance to the voices of youth in our culture feels surprising, given that I was briefly one of those voices decades earlier. Yet perhaps not so surprising when I recognize that it took me until years after the fact to appreciate the impact movies I was in had on the youth of the day. I've not forgotten the shock and disorientation I felt the first time I walked into a mall and had to quickly leave as I was surrounded by scores of my teenage contemporaries.

"Young people change the world, Sammy," I say. "Old guys like me are too comfortable or trying too hard to hold on to what we have. Kids really shouldn't listen to grown-ups."

My son can barely be bothered to reply, "Don't worry, I don't."

The midafternoon siesta is alive and well in the north of Spain. For several hours during the worst heat of the day, stores are shuttered, services cease, and the streets are deserted while the local population retreat to their homes for lunch and a nap. A stranger passing through and not accustomed to such a sensible ritual could be excused for thinking he had stumbled onto a post-apocalyptic film set. In the already sleepy village of Uterga, a tabby cat strolling across the narrow street without a care is the only sign of life. In Muruzábal, a dead sparrow in the gutter under a glaring sun takes on ominous overtones. Obanos has cobbled streets, stone buildings, and one of the Camino's most iconic Romanesque churches—purportedly linked to the Knights Templar. It invites attention, but with everything shut up tight, we don't even break stride.

Leaving town, we pass a grove of olive trees.

"What is it about manipulation?" Sam says at last. "Especially when you can see it happening, but it somehow makes you even more obsessed. It's really messed up."

"Mmmm."

We pass a grove of almond trees.

"And knowing it's, like, all about control, it…it…"

"It doesn't help?"

"No!" Sam almost shouts. "It's so fucked up."

We bisect a field of sinister-looking sunflowers.

"You're not in Kansas anymore, Dorothy."

"Huh?"

"Relationships, Sammy. They're complicated."

We walk through the first of La Rioja's soon-to-be-ubiquitous vineyards. Then a cornfield, then more cut wheat. We talk bullying.

"That's just about insecurity, Sam. And fear. Masking it. Turning it around, trying to get power."

"Maybe." Sam is skeptical. "You say everything is fear."

"It usually is."

Sam wonders if he is working through this break-up more than The Ex back home.

"I mean, I'm sure I'm thinking and talking about it more than her."

On this afternoon, it would be difficult, I agree silently, for anyone on the planet to be talking about it more.

"Maybe," I say softly.

I'm humbled and touched that my son would trust me enough to share what's in his heart, but when we at last come upon Puente la Reina, I hear myself groan, "Oh, thank God!" with perhaps a bit too much relief.

"I wouldn't call it fun"

426 miles to Santiago

Sam and I have reached a détente regarding our start time each day. Perhaps it's because all three of my children were up with the sun when they were little, or maybe it's just that I'm getting old, but I am now firmly in the habit of rising early, despite how tired I might be or when I go to bed. Sam, on the other hand, will sleep until the crack of noon unless awoken. As the heat of the August afternoon makes the walking much more challenging—and it is only getting hotter as we move west—we have agreed that 8:00 a.m. is an appropriate time to get moving.

The conversation went like this:

Me: (scolding) "Look, this is what we're doing. If you don't want to do it, go home. If you do, then we have to get going each day."

Sam: (sulking) "Fine."

This leaves me with at least an hour each morning to myself. And this morning, there is an attractive café on the cobbled main street of Puente la Reina. I sit out front with my café con leche and tortilla Española as the sun emerges over my shoulder, casting its rays directly down the narrow east/west heading lane. For a few minutes, everything is illuminated in soft golden light. As the earth rotates, shadows take back over Calle Mayor until only the belfry of La Iglesia de Santiago retains a warm glow of morning sun. When a street sweeper rattles down the lane, it kicks up clouds of dust, and I put my hand over my coffee. A half dozen pilgrims come and go. They're stretching, chatting, grabbing breakfast to take away and hitting the road. The street sweeper returns from the other

51

direction, kicking up more dust, most of which still hasn't settled from its first pass. I once again cover my coffee. As the sweeper recedes, backlit in a fog of its own creation, I can't shake the image of Pigpen from the Charlie Brown cartoon, who was always engulfed in a cloud of his own dust.

We're out the door a little after 9:00 a.m., just over an hour late—which is better than I thought we'd do. The road takes us onto the bridge that gave Puente la Reina its name. As we cross, the sun over our left shoulder casts long shadows before us on the stone footpath. Now that the Camino has turned due west, we will meet our elongated, live-action cameos each morning.

We cut across the highway, pick up a dirt trail, and begin to climb. Setting out each morning, I generally keep quiet, knowing Sam still has a lot to process regarding The Ex. And he'll start up soon enough. It is as if thoughts and feelings had been gathering overnight at the foot of his bed and upon waking announce, "I'm glad you're up, Sam. I've got a lot to talk to you about."

In a few hours, Sam is usually talked out on the topic for the day, and as we pass more wheat, he sums up today's session with, "All too often, pain is the price of wisdom." I wonder where he heard such a line, one that sounds both wise and banal enough to be printed on a greeting card. I later look it up to see if it is attributed to anyone specific and find nothing.

A group of bikers passes us, and Sam calls out the obligatory *Mal Camino!* as they kick dirt up in our faces. The sun is increasingly becoming a factor on the walk—still midmorning, it burns down. Unripe blackberries grow from prickly bushes lining a trail that continues to get steeper. Sam pushes on ahead, powered by nineteen-year-old legs and heartache. A large gorge has been cut into the trail by rains that are nowhere in sight, and I have to pick my way. At the ridge, another field of cut wheat stretches toward the Pico de Europa mountains to the north.

In the village of Mañeru, a cluster of small children and an old man sit on a blanket spread in the middle of the cobblestone street in front of an attractive stone house. I step over the blanket, and the children wish me a *"Buen Camino."* I hustle on to get Sam in sight again. Through vineyards and olive groves, I sweat my way into the medieval village of Cirauqui.

Sam is already seated on the ground, leaning against a stone building under an overflowing window box of white and purple petunias. He is more than a little relieved to see me, not because he has missed me or was worried, but because an old man with hands clasped behind his back, wearing a cardigan sweater buttoned up against the summer heat, is standing over him, attempting conversation. I greet the old man, and he quizzes me on what we are doing. His accent is so thick that it is difficult for me to understand him. He soon grows frustrated with me, waves a hand in my face, and shuffles over to the bakery across the tiny village square.

We get a bad coffee from a vending machine and meet a young Canadian couple making the Camino for their honeymoon. Then Ryan, one of the two Americans we met with the edgy Irishman on our second day, appears. Ryan is quick to offer up his story. Twenty-nine, from Colorado, quit his job, searching for . . . then shrugs.

Ryan is affable and direct in the uncomplicated way that is so easy to detect in Americans when they are out of America. As he is telling us about the Eurail Pass he's secured for after the Camino, the old man in the cardigan returns from the bakery, paper bag in his arms. Perhaps not recognizing me from moments earlier, or just having decided on another shot at conversation, he steps in front of me again. In the universal method of talking very loudly in order to be understood, he begins to shout at me while standing very close. I try not to recoil from his bitter coffee breath. I understand nothing of what the man says but make a show of knitting my brow. I add an earnest head-nod. This seems to encourage him, and he keeps talking. I offer my hand. He is pleased by

ANDREW MCCARTHY

this. His meaty mitt grabs mine, and he says something else. I laugh. He laughs. He then moves off, clearly satisfied by the encounter.

Still seated on the ground, Sam looks up. "What the hell was he saying?"

"I have no idea."

We pass through a Gothic arch in the town's ancient fortification wall and make our way back into the fields over the finest remnant of Roman road on the Camino, and then over a single span of Roman bridge. We cross the once dangerous Río Salado. In the twelfth century, Navarran men were said to lie in wait to skin the hide of any passing pilgrim's horse that drank from the deadly waters. Today, what little water trickles by looks fine, and with no trouble in sight, we swig from our water bottles and walk on.

There is no shade. We pass more olive groves and vineyards. At a fork in the dirt trail, there is no yellow arrow to be seen. Two couples are already staring down at their unfurled maps and guidebooks, looking left and right, then down again, trying to decide in which direction to go. Sam pulls out his phone. Without breaking stride, he says, "We're off the trail. It's this way," and he makes a sharp left onto a small dirt adjunct.

"How do you know, Sammy?"

"Snapchat."

He shows me his phone. His avatar of a small green man with a wide-brimmed black hat is off the clearly labeled "Camino Frances" (another name for this particular trail of the Camino).

"Seriously?"

"I've been following it the whole way." He shrugs.

"Then why the hell am I carrying these heavy books?"

"Dude, I've been asking that myself."

The small trail leads us directly to a yellow arrow, and we're on track again. We call back to the others, still bent over their maps, and they hurry in our direction.

Talk turns to the smoking of pot, and the taking of hallucinogens.

54

Sam has experimented with the latter and indulges in the former more than makes me comfortable. I had my own experience with both at his age and went on to become a raging alcoholic, so I have strong opinions on the subject.

"I mean, I'm sure I'll do acid or mushrooms a few more times," he says, "but it's not something I'd make a habit of. They're not like that."

"I remember a David Bowie concert where I took mushrooms," I tell him. "It started to get very weird, and I ended up just wandering out of the theater in the middle of the show. By the time I got home, I was having terrible hallucinations. I turned on the TV and David Letterman had horns. It went on and on. I just hid under the covers all night."

"I know, you've told me that."

That I have pounded my children with cautionary tales regarding my own use of drugs and alcohol does little, I know, to ensure that they will steer clear of them. Drugs and alcohol exist on a slippery slope of experimentation and lessons learned that all people coming of age must navigate for themselves.

"And I left before he had played 'Changes.' I never did hallucinogens again."

"Didn't stop you from drinking, though," Sam says.

"No, it didn't." I encourage his thoughts on the matter.

"It's just, sometimes pot gets your thoughts going, like you really see between things."

"But when you come down, are those thoughts still insightful?"

"Sometimes." What I hear all too distinctly is the sense of thrill that the topic elicits. It's chasing that dragon that leads the young to dare greatness and tempt destruction in equal measure—this thought does nothing to appease me.

And then three young bikers race past. One of them, a young woman clad in tight biking shorts and a small tank top, has long blond hair flying loose behind her. Sam's habitual call of "*Mal Camino!*" is absent.

At the village of Lorca, we sit on the ground in the uninspired town square and eat jamón serrano and salami from our packs. A kitten approaches Sam with caution. Sam offers up a piece of meat, and soon the cat is sitting in his lap, eating out of his hand. Sam has one eye on the tabby and one on the attractive biker who passed us on the trail. She's across the square, lying down with her head in the lap of one of her two male friends.

As we head out of town, Sam says, "That biker girl was pretty," in a tone so casual and disinterested that it would be easy for his remark to slip past unnoticed. But I hear his words like the first gasp of air from a suffocating man.

"She was," I say with matching indifference.

The trail parallels the N-111 highway and traffic races past. It's a discouraging feeling to look over and see cars that will accomplish in minutes a journey that will take us hours to complete. I allow myself a moment of wondering, "What the hell am I doing, anyway?" I keep the thought to myself and turn over my shoulder when I hear a sound. The blond young woman and her two friends are bouncing up the trail.

"Watch out, Sam. Here comes your girlfriend."

Sam turns and sees them coming. "All right, all right. It's a little soon," he grumbles. Then Sam, who has taken his shirt off in the heat, steps off the trail to let them pass.

The girl's head swivels toward Sam as she squeezes by on the narrow trail. "*Buen Camino,*" she purrs.

"*Buen Camino!*" Sam calls after her.

We march on through the heat of the afternoon over stark terrain, passing under the highway, and the church spires of Estella come into view.

"I'm glad I'm doing this," Sam says out of sweating silence. "I wouldn't call it fun, but it's satisfying."

I can't deny the feeling of relief I experience in hearing this, but before I can reply, Sam continues.

"I'm glad to talk to you. It's good."

I'm so touched by this simple and earnest acknowledgment that you could knock me over with a feather. But then, I am so tired from today's fourteen-plus-mile walk in the heat that you could knock me over with a feather anyway.

"I can't talk to you"

413 miles to Santiago

After an hour on my back with my feet up the wall, I've recovered enough to explore my surroundings. Estella began life—like most of the towns we pass through—as a response to the needs of pilgrims marching to Santiago. A textile industry quickly blossomed. Beautiful churches and institutions were erected. But where money flows, trouble follows. In 1328, a large portion of the town's Jewish population was massacred in a riot; the rest were forced to convert during the Inquisition. A castle was destroyed. The walls of a cloister were torn down. The plague halved the population in the fourteenth century. Nestled on the banks of the Rio Ega, "Estella la Bella" has a checkered past.

I find its present similarly conflicted. The cobbled main street with centuries-old buildings, the medieval bridge with children feeding ducks in the gentle river below, the flowing fountains and buzzing popula-tion all contribute to my quick decision that I need a rest day here. But walking on, I find a dingy main square, an overabundance of graffiti. Numerous storefronts are shuttered, *En Alquiler* signs peel from taped-over windows. A chubby boy in a Ramones T-shirt kicks me a soccer ball, inviting me to play, while nearby drunken men sing the afternoon away in a sour-smelling bar. It's a tough place to figure.

Whatever mood I'm in, Estella's contradictions illuminate some of my own paradoxes of character, and I begin to see my wife's occasional frus-trations with my temperament in a way I hadn't before. While I find it only natural to reconcile conflicting aspects of my own personality—my desire for intimacy and need for solitude, my interest in public success and my wanting to hide—such seesaw leanings can, I grasp at this moment, confound those closest to me.

Inside the Iglesia San Miguel, I try to ignore the thick, musty scent. The silence in the deserted building is oppressive. A lone ray of light through a small stained-glass window casts a tiny glow of luminous green and red on the pew in front of me. I watch the light creep across the wood. It grows in intensity before the waning sun goes behind a cloud and the colors evaporate. I'm the only one who saw it.

I feel my transience acutely this evening. Melancholy is a feeling I rarely get a chance to indulge in back home, when life demands more concrete, more active, responses. Here, on the road, there is space.

Sam and I eat; our talk is of no real consequence. I feel a pang of responsibility that I engage him more, challenge him more, parent him, guide him, provide wisdom or insight. My mood doesn't support such assertion. Nor do I feel equipped in this moment to simply be his friend. I let it be. Sam heads off for ice cream, to bum cigarettes, to call his friends back home. I wander the shadowy streets. Taking one last pass through the main square on my way to bed, I see Sam on the phone, sitting on the worn steps of La Iglesia de San Pedro de la Rúa, talking intently, private in public. We're just two people passing through.

With the dawn of a new day, such indulgent whimsy has no place. Yet another street sweeper anchors me in the here and now, spraying disinfectant all over my shoes while I sip coffee at a table out front of an empty café on the Plaza de Santiago. I am ready to move on from Estella la Bella.

The way out of town is through roundabouts and past ugly, 1970s-era yellow brick apartment blocks on Calle Zalatambor. "They're kind of cool," Sam says of the European-style housing. "I've never seen them before." Just a mile up the trail, we come upon one of the Camino's oddities, a fountain dispensing free red wine from a spigot on the side of the local Irache Winery. Sam dips his finger and tastes. "Man, that's sour. I don't think I get wine." He shrugs.

"I didn't either... at first."

Moving off again, Sam is discussing The Ex and in context mentions a young woman we know from back home, how she would perhaps like to hook up with him. I recoil at the almost incestuous seeming nature of the suggestion.

"That's gross, Sam."

"I can't talk to you or treat you like a person if you're going to react like that," Sam scolds me.

In order to avoid contact with the N-111 and in looking for relief from the sun after our typical, hours-late start, I lead us on an alternate route that climbs the lower slope of Mountejurra, tracking west through an attractive forest of evergreen and brushwood. Because it is slightly longer, it's an infrequently used portion of the old Camino, but the natural and twisting trail through the trees offers walking in welcome shade. Its meandering course encourages conversation in a similar unguided manner. Sam talks at length and in great detail about weight lifting, his former passion. We discuss Coke in cans vs. bottles, ketogenic diets, rap music—"It's a real shame you don't like it." Sam shakes his head. Then, "I wonder when the Oscars will begin offering awards to nonbinary performers."

"Wait," I say. "Did I miss a topic change?"

"No, I just thought of it."

We've encountered no one on this old adjunct of the Camino and at a clearing sit down directly on the trail for a break. The view stretches over the wheat fields and the snaking highway and the main trail in the valley below and out to the mountains in the north. A distant church bell rings out twelve times. We have a clear view of the tenth-century castle crowning the conical mountain of Monjardin. "Good call to take this route," Sam says between bites of chorizo.

The tranquility of the moment is interrupted by the sounds of Bob Dylan's "Like a Rolling Stone," being sung a cappella by the edgy Irishman—whose name we have learned is Kiren, but whom we have begun to refer to simply as "Irish." For a moment, it appears as if he will charge right over us, then Irish stops abruptly at our feet. He has been up all night. The reason is a little vague. We shield our eyes from the sun as we look up at him looming over us. Then, in midsentence, he stomps off, his departure as sudden as his arrival. The loud and tuneless singing is picked up where it was left off and is a long time in fading.

Eventually, Sam turns to me. "Irish has got a lot going on."

We encounter him again a few miles later in the village of Luquin, a typical hill town with winding streets emanating from the church. The sleepy place has the enticement of a municipal swimming pool. Sam and I are considering the possibility of a refreshing dip in the midday heat when Irish appears from the nearby café, brandishing a ticket for the pool.

"I'm going to take a swim," he boasts.

"Where'd you get that ticket?" Sam asks.

Irish turns on him, glaring. "Here, take it." He presses the ticket into Sam's hand and charges off down the trail.

"Is he on drugs?" Sam asks.

"Maybe he just needs sleep," I say without conviction.

With the exception of the first day hiking over the Pyrenees, where there was little support, there has usually been no more than a few miles between villages or towns offering a break, or at least a distraction along the way. The next eight miles to our goal of Los Arcos is over dirt tracks through rolling fields of wheat, scorched sunflowers, and little else. The mind wanders. I recall a dream I had a few nights earlier in which I played the cello with great ease. It's a pleasant recollection—one only imaginable for me in a dream—and made space for by the total absence of anything other than the obligation to walk on. Sam has been recalling a dream of a different sort.

"Think that girl was with that guy?"

We have not mentioned the blond biker since she passed us yesterday, yet I know instantly about whom he is speaking.

"I got the impression that the two guys were the couple, and she was the friend."

"Yeah, me too. Think we'll see her again?"

"She's gone, Sammy. Halfway to Santiago by now."

Sam is silent.

"But look," I go on, "that was actually an important relationship for you."

"Huh?"

"She let you know you've still got a pulse."

Sam looks over at me, checking to see if I'm serious. When I shrug, he frowns, plugs in his earbuds, and marches ahead. By his air guitar I assume he's listening to John Mayer. I tune in to some Bob Marley, hoping to ease my grinding way.

Often, while traveling, I abstain from listening to music, preferring to not imprint a familiar soundtrack on a new experience. And there are different schools of thinking on listening to music along The Way. Some purists consider it anathema to distract themselves from what the Camino might be telling them at any given moment. But with a mind that loops and gets caught in eddies more often than I'd care for anyway, I've come to regard my own process as not so precious. There are as many paths to purification as there are walkers along the road. I'll take whatever help I can get on a blistering afternoon.

At a small cluster of shade trees by the side of the trail, I catch up with Sam, who is chatting with Ryan and Oyster Bay (aka Chris). Although they're a decade older than Sam, he's taken to calling them The Boys.

They're accompanied now by a Hungarian woman with sad eyes named Erika. Sam has dropped his pack and bummed a cigarette. He puffs with contentment. They all appear cool and calm in the shade. I stand sweating profusely.

"They saw Irish," Sam says.

"Yeah, he passed a while ago," Chris says. "Seemed kind of worked up."

"Dad, did you go to Finisterre last time you walked the Camino?"

"I didn't."

"The Boys here are talking about going."

Fifty miles and three days' walk past Santiago de Compostela lies Finisterre, literally translated as "the end of land." A spit of rocky terrain above the Atlantic Ocean, at one time believed to be the westernmost reach of Europe, it is not far from where the Apostle James's boat was said to have come ashore. While officially not a part of the Camino, many pilgrims feel the pull to make the extra walk. I never did.

"Santiago will be enough for me, boys," I say. "If I make it."

"We'll make it." Sam stubs out his cigarette.

The off-handed remark is not lost on me.

Sam hoists his pack, and we march on. At one point we lose the yellow arrows, and Sam sets us right with his little green man on Snapchat. A small dust twister swirls up in front of us. We arrive in Los Arcos, a town of just over a thousand, in the middle of the siesta. Everything is boarded up tight.

The town evolved as a crossroads supporting trading posts and still retains that transient, edgy quality. A hot wind blows, and the smell of the baking earth is distinct. Two motorcycles roar down the two-lane highway on the outskirts of town. Old men with canes watch from benches with disapproval. A few teens play handball against a wall. Los Arcos possesses two churches. One rings out the hour, then five minutes later, the other does the same. Inquiring about a possible place for dinner, I'm told there are four restaurants in town; three of them have closed down. There is little of the architectural appeal many Camino towns possess. Charm here is elusive.

In most villages, Pilgrims tend to congregate in one area. In Los Arcos, that area is the Plaza de Santa María. And it's there that I find Irish seated at a café table alone, continuing his Bob Dylan concert from earlier, now singing "The Times They Are a-Changin'" in full voice. A half dozen pilgrims at nearby tables keep their eyes on their beer. I duck my head and keep moving. Turning a corner, I find Sam, just hanging up his phone, eating his ice cream.

"You have a good walk around?" I ask.

"I can't believe people live here," he says, shaking his head. "I mean..."

If I hadn't heard his earlier assurance about our making it to Santiago, I might be more concerned about this place offering enough enticement for Sam. But hearing him vocalize his casual commitment has relaxed me in a way I didn't know I was still seeking. We are partners on the road. That we have been for some days now should have been clear to me—but my preexisting feelings of responsibility and overattentiveness have prevented me from seeing what's right in front of me. I've been conscious to remain actively positive with Sam about all aspects of the Camino up to this point—which in most instances has been easy to do—but I'm at a loss on how to spin this place. Dropping any pretense, I say, "It's a shithole, Sam."

"I'm just a little angry"

399 miles to Santiago

"Don't make me police you. You're an adult. If you don't want to do this, then don't. If you do, this is what is required!" It's the same speech I give most mornings, but perhaps because I slept so poorly, or maybe because the bad coffee at the grimy café was served by a sour barman, but today my tirade is delivered with more spleen than usual. I have no patience for Sam's morning sloth. I can hear myself but am unable to hold my frustration in check.

This was the main accusation that my family leveled against my father—that he just couldn't stop. He would explode and storm out of a room, only to return moments later to continue, to add another point, to throw another venomous dart, to scatter-bomb the room. Here in Los Arcos, there is only one room, so the dramatic exit and reentrance isn't possible. If I were on the receiving end of this rant, as Sam is, I'd bury my head under the covers too.

As I write this, I realize I am being perhaps unfair to my father, painting a one-dimensional portrait of him. My dad could also be a wildly charming man; he was a natural salesman, and popular around town. He was our Little League coach. He told us often that he loved us. It's simply that his anger, to those of us who knew him between our four walls, dominated our experience of him. The potential for an explosion was ever present. It has taken a long time to report on this experience without a reactionary gasp and hunching of the shoulders.

On the way out of town, we pass a cemetery. Above the entrance is posted a sign—*You are what I once was and will be what I am now.*

"That's not really helpful at the moment," I say aloud.

Just beyond a power grid, a lone bird in midair is flapping its wings furiously—but perpendicular to the ground, simply maintaining its position in the still air. So much effort expended to get nowhere—I push away the cheap metaphor for my own life.

"This is the worst coffee I've had the entire trip," Sam says, and dumps the contents of his cup on the dirt trail.

"We just have to get away from this town," I mutter.

We walk in silence, as we often do early on, before Sam begins talking about The Ex. But there's an added tension today.

Perhaps because of my father's frequent outbursts growing up, my reaction to explosive anger throughout my life has tended to be one of withdrawal, often taking days before risking emotional reemergence. That I am the culprit in this case instead of the recipient only compounds the problem.

"I'm sorry, Sam. I shouldn't have gotten so upset. You don't deserve it, and it's not helpful—to either of us."

A rare morning drizzle has stopped, and the air still clings to a crispness that the heat of the day will soon swallow. It takes another half hour on the trail, walking in lockstep, but Sam finally begins to speak.

"I'm just a little angry, Dad," Sam says.

"I know, Sam. And again, I'm sorry."

"What? Oh. No, that's fine." He waves his hand. My son has always been much more able than me to release reactive emotion and move on.

But apparently the cause of Sam's upset this morning has a more culturally relevant, but equally incendiary, root—there was a post on Instagram that Sam perceived was intended to make him jealous.

(This is the portion of the narrative in which the older person proclaims how grateful he is that he did not come of age amid the current thorny thicket of social media, with its real-time dangers of impulsivity.)

"Just a picture. I fucking hate jealousy," he says.

"It's pretty debilitating," I agree.

"And that I fall for it. I know it was posted for me to see. It just makes me so angry."

I mention the five stages of grief, and anger being one of them.

"Yeah, but I thought I'd gotten through—"

"It ain't a straight line, Sammy."

And Sam's phone rings. One of his friends is calling from back home, where it is near dawn.

"Toby never sleeps," Sam says, silencing the phone.

"Take it, Sammy. Get a different perspective."

Sam sprints ahead. I watch as he goes, his arms beginning to wave as he vents, his walk taking on a strut—at home in himself on the trail. Seeing this, my mood lifts.

The heat of the day has taken hold. The path climbs, revealing neat rows of vineyards that speak to an order my thoughts resist. I recognize the moment I become hungry and soon after feel its resulting stress. My mind churns, looking for something on which to latch itself. At the crest of the hill, all but obscured behind overgrown scrub, sits a small chapel containing a statue of the Virgin. The statue has been moved several times to other, sometimes distant locations, only to mysteriously return to this spot again and again, seemingly of its own accord.

The trail drops precipitously now. Emerging from a bend, I come upon several pairs of boots that have been discarded by the side of the trail. Further on I see a drawstring bag filled with clothes. We have reached the point on the Camino in which people begin to discard what they can no longer abide.

I think of my wife, and tears begin to roll down my cheeks. I don't even know why. Love, I suppose. Latching hold of easy Camino metaphors, I'm grateful that we have, like the mysterious Virgin, chosen to emotionally return to each other over and over again rather than let our bond be discarded by the side of the trail when it felt too heavy to bear.

Then my phone is ringing. Dolores is on the line. "I just thought I'd say 'hi,'" she says and can hear me laugh. "What's funny?"

"I married a witch," I say. "I was just thinking about you."

"I know you were," she says.

In the low clearing of a valley, hills rise steeply around a lone farmer working a small vineyard, and I come upon Sam sitting atop a single picnic table positioned to receive the afternoon shade from a few tall and thin pine trees. He is tossing M&M's up into the air and catching them in his mouth. I'm reminded of our first camping trip together, when Sam was eight. We went on a five-mile hike to a lake in New York's Catskill Mountains. At one point, Sam sat down on the trail and announced, "This is the worst day of my life." But things improved dramatically for him the next morning when I realized I had forgotten breakfast and we were forced to survive on M&M'S.

"This is a nice spot," I call out and let my pack crash to the ground.

"It is indeed a fine hologram of reality." Sam has theories on our time/space continuum that go far beyond my here-and-now comprehension. Walking through open spaces has proven to be the perfect place on which to expound on his musings, but they continue to prove beyond my grasp.

Then, switching gears without warning, Sam says, "I'd like to stop thinking about it."

I know he is talking about The Ex. "I don't blame you," I say. "You will when you do."

Sam rolls his eyes and fires up a cigarette I didn't know he'd mooched. I lie on my back and look up into the trees. This is the kind of tranquil respite the Camino provides at unexpected moments, one best taken advantage of when found. Sam practices smoking with different grips.

"Who's the best smoker in the movies?"

"Humphrey Bogart," I say without pause.

"What movies was he in?"

"Watch *Casablanca*."

"You like that movie, don't you?"

"Best movie ever."

"Anybody more recent?"

"You can't smoke in the movies nowadays."

"Unless you're the villain," Sam adds.

"True."

We're silent for a time.

"There are people in my generation who will tell you that I smoked a mean cigarette in *St. Elmo's Fire*. Not that I should be encouraging such things."

"Should I see that movie?"

"No need," I tell him. For a long time, I kept my life as a young movie star out of my children's world—until a decade ago, when we were on a road trip. At a diner in Wyoming, I was out with Sam as the others napped. Our waitress cornered me, going on at length about a movie in which I had appeared. There was no escape. Sam watched the encounter with wide eyes. When, after a dozen photos and an autograph, the waitress finally left, I turned to Sam. "How was that for you, kiddo?" I asked.

"Oh, Dad," my nine-year-old son said, his eyes brimming, "I was so proud."

I realized in that instant that I had done everything wrong in excluding my children from such a huge part of my experience. From then on, it's all been fair game.

We climb the hill to the walled town of Viana, long a refuge for pilgrims. Its colonnades, flowing fountains, and outdoor cafés are all the stuff a pilgrim like me craves. On our way down the cobbled Calle Mayor, we stop for a bite and quickly decide to abort Logroño, still several miles off, and stay here for the night.

Then things start to go south.

Irish appears from nowhere and sits down at our table. Wild eyed, he's intrigued we have chosen to stay the night.

"Might even be worth a rest day here," I say.

"Rest for a whole day?" Irish is incredulous at the notion.

"Yeah, maybe."

He jumps up as if he might catch something from us and races off. But soon he hurries past again, first in one direction and then the other, ignoring us each time.

Then the most expensive plate of jamón ibérico we've ordered to date (and we've ordered a lot) is mealy and overly fatty. Then the dear hotel at which I have decided to splurge—which, from what I can tell by the deserted lobby and restaurant, is nearly empty—puts us in a room at the back with a tiny window onto an airshaft and refuses to consider shifting us.

"We are complete, sir." The unctuous youth behind the counter smirks.

Granted, we are smelly pilgrims, but my credit card is as good as the next tourist's. After a half hour on a sagging bed with my feet up the wall, I turn to Sam.

"Want to get out of here?"

"Now?"

"Yeah."

"And go where?"

"Logroño."

Sam is through the door without another word.

It's well past 5:00 p.m., and the heat of the day is still up. Skipping town on Calle Fuente Vieja, through the medieval stone arch Portal San Felices, we drop down past the backs of houses and waste ground and abandoned factories, cross the N-111, and make our way into the wetlands of the Pantano de la Cañas. The low-lying area was notorious for witches' covens in the sixteenth century. Today, it's a bird sanctuary. For reasons that are unclear, Sam begins to speak in an Australian accent—and will not stop. By the time we recross the N-111, I am ready to throw myself in front of any oncoming vehicle.

We pass scraggily vineyards and power lines. Factories. Car dealerships. The outskirts of the city. At a graffiti-covered highway underpass beside a drainage ditch, Sam begins to slow and then sits down suddenly on the asphalt. When he was a small child, Sam suffered not-infrequent sugar crashes. I can recognize one when I see one and walk back to him, offering one of the secret stash of protein bars I have kept for just such an emergency. He gnaws it hungrily, silently. I breathe beside him.

"Better," he says at last.

I reach out and rub his shoulder. He nods softly, gratefully. We sit together in the gutter as thousands upon thousands of dandelion puffs, backlit by the evening sun, float in the air like dancing diamonds.

"It's just so fucking far"

382 miles to Santiago

Crossing the Rio Ebro and making our way to the old city in the last light of the lingering summer evening, we experience the thrill of arrival. Unlike our mistimed entrance into most villages during siesta, we hit Logroño during the evening paseo, when it seems the entire city is on parade. Girls wearing skinny jeans and munching chips strut past boys in football jerseys. Lovers amble hand in hand. Old folks fill benches. Children chase. After a solid week and close to a hundred miles of walking, I am ready for a day of rest. This university town of 150,000 is the place for it.

Over the years, I thought I remembered it all, but I've come to see that with the exception of the random mental snapshots lodged in my brain from my last trip, filed away without regard for their importance, so much appears new to me this time. Even the feelings I attribute to my first Camino, I see now, were altered by repeated recollection to fit a narrative of my conscious or unconscious choosing. What did I see and experience so long ago? While emotional truth remains, the facts appear to be largely blurred or forgotten. And I have no clear recollection of Logroño.

Sitting at an outdoor café along the pedestrian Calle Portales at the Plaza del Mercado on a warm summer night, looking up at the baroque towers of the Iglesia de Santa María la Redonda, storks nesting in its belfry, I watch the parade of humanity. Sam has wandered off, and I have taken a seat.

One of the most important things in making travel palatable over the long term is the establishing of some form of routine. Since our life on the Camino has all to do with movement rather than situation, I decide that while we're stopped here, a single, familiar place is primary for peace of mind. The wicker chair, the small round table—there is nothing special about my choice. There are similar cafés on either side of the one in which I sit, but this one, chosen almost at random, will be my base of operations for the next thirty-six hours. Sam circles past a few times, reporting on sights and goings-on. Only when he suggests we get some ice cream do I rouse myself.

But the simple satisfactions of the night are gone with the new day. Sam wakes edgy and irritable. My eldest son has always been most comfortable while in motion. Stagnation is a devil's garden.

Impatient with his restlessness, I suggest he go and find a gym and work out.

"I found one, but I don't know how to talk to them."

"Just hold up your money and make a weight-lifting gesture. They'll get it."

"Fine."

Sam walks out, only to return a moment later.

"I don't have any money."

I do my laundry in the sink, then drift through the old town. I'm dumbfounded by how long I can watch a mime outside a church. I go to buy a shirt but am too tired to try it on. I'm lulled by an old woman playing the accordion on Calle Laurel. I return to my café and sit.

By the following morning, we're both ready to walk. Grabbing my stick and hat, I glance at myself in the full-length mirror by the door. My sweat-stained shirt, fraying shorts, dusty shoes, all markers of pride while on the Camino, appear to me here, in this air-conditioned comfort, as somewhat silly. When I pass the attractive woman at the front desk, the feeling is one of vulnerability, even rawness.

While on the trail, such unmasked feeling sits comfortably accessible and welcome, allowing easier connection with other pilgrims, encouraging a directness in communication. But here in the city, with that usual protective layer of emotional insulation temporarily burned off by the road, a pilgrim can feel ill-equipped to be interacting with "civilians" in the veiled dance of society.

Heading out of town, following brass scallop shells inlaid into the sidewalk along Calle Ruavieja, an old woman calls down to us from a balcony, "*Buen Camino!*" Then so does a thin woman with a thinner dog on Calle Barriocepo. Then an old man at the Puerta del Revellín does the same. The phrase, especially when offered up with such affection, is beginning to grow on me. It's good to be walking again and reminded that there is a legacy in what we're doing, that we are a part of something.

Outside a large police station surrounded by strong fortification, a woman bites her nails and paces, while the man beside her whispers into his phone with urgency. I offer a silent prayer of thanks that Sam and I walk so free.

Over railroad tracks and under the highway, through a park and into wetlands and around a reservoir, parallel to the highway and through fields of wheat, we walk until vineyards reassert their dominance over the landscape. A paraglider floats over the hills to the south. Apple trees briefly line the trail.

Sam talks of the temptations of ayahuasca. "The Boys, Ryan and Chris, are talking about going to Peru to do it." Then he brings up a friend of ours in Ireland. "And Dolores's friend, Conor, he said it changed his life."

I just listen. Then Sam mentions someone named Raya.

"Who's Raya?"

"It's a celebrity dating app."

"How the hell do you know about all this stuff?" I ask.

"Uh...'cause I'm in the world?"

In the attractive village of Navarrete, we stop at a café. We sit too long, and when I try to rouse Sam, he looks at me. "It's just so fucking far, Dad."

I have nothing to add to that.

He's quiet for a minute, then—"I don't know what I have to rush back for, though."

The church bells ring out eleven times.

On the way out of the village, Sam hands me one of his earbuds.

"What is it?"

"Kendrick Lamar."

I groan. "Really?"

"Oh, come on."

I place the earbud. "King Kunta" plays. I find it irritating, and impossible to decipher the lyrics. The song ends, and I pull the bud from my ear.

"Forget it." Sam grabs it back.

"What? I listened. It's just not my thing."

"It wasn't even finished."

"Oh, I thought—"

"Bullshit. Never mind."

He storms off. Watching Sam charge away down the trail, I'm enraged by his flash of adolescent judgment and air of superiority, the disregard with which he's treated me. I ignore my own attitude of dismissal, the intolerant righteousness with which I handed back the earbud. The moment doesn't reflect especially well on either of us. The unremitting sun doesn't help.

On a small hill out of town, my backpack begins a rhythmic creak with each placement of my left foot. With every step, I grow in irritation. I put the Eagles' greatest hits on my headphones in order to drown the sound. It's not lost on me that I have chosen what is perhaps the ultimate "old white guy" record in reaction to my son's judgment.

I've been feeling guilty this morning, leaving Dolores holding the bag back home while I saunter across Spain and so, for no reason other than that offense is the best defense, I grow irritated at my wife.

"The hell with everyone," I say aloud and stomp on over a dusty track through yet another fucking vineyard.

A large shadow passes on the trail in front of me. A massive bird glides slowly overhead and arcs back around me.

"Cue the goddamn vulture." I shake my head in disgust.

I reach over and pick a still unripe grape from a vine. It tastes like a sour pellet. Now I'm just looking to make myself feel bad. It doesn't matter. It's what I want to do, and the hell with you if you don't like it. The intensity of the sun and midday heat are not on my side. There are still more than ten miles to walk today. I forgot to fill my water bottle in Naverrete.

Ahead, a small road cuts across the path. A yellow arrow on a telephone pole points west. Nailed to the post just above the arrow is a hand-painted sign—Guillermo's Taxi—and then a phone number. I look ahead to the trail through vineyards stretching to the horizon.

"And fuck you, Guillermo."

I have now begun to talk to myself out loud. It doesn't matter; I'm the only one worth listening to anyway. I may be getting sunstroke.

I come upon Sam hours later at a picnic area fenced in by the side of the trail. Immature trees and tables attempt relief from the sun. This kind of gesture, offering the pilgrim comfort along The Way, is new since my last Camino. Sam is seated on the rail in the gazebo, smoking.

"I'm sorry, Dad," he says after I drop my pack. "I was just frustrated."

"I'm sorry, too, Sammy." I reach out my hand for the earbud. "Sometimes I'm just an asshole. Here, let me listen again."

"Stop. It doesn't matter."

We let it drop. I sit and sweat. Sam hands me his bottle of water.

"What do you think about going to Finisterre?" he asks.

"You?"

"Yeah."

"Might be nice."

"It's three days past Santiago?"

"Yup."

Sam nods.

"This thing just upsets me."

I know he is talking about The Ex. "Understandable," I say.

Sam pulls out a pack of cigarettes and lights another.

"Where'd you get the pack?"

"No one will let me bum them anymore."

I laugh. "I thought you were quitting on this trip."

Sam shrugs. "Whatever."

"Well, at least now you can chain-smoke."

"Look, I'll become a complete Buddha of self-mastery by the time we finish, but one thing at a time." He inhales deeply.

"I'm not a pilgrim"

364 miles to Santiago

Under bright fluorescent lights at the empty Bar Naxara in the riverside town of Najera, I order breakfast. The disgruntled, exhausted man behind the counter sets to work on my coffee without comment.

"How are you, sir?" I ask, using the formal conjugation of the verb.

He turns and considers me, as if making a momentous decision. He tells me how little he sleeps, how much work he must do.

"*Entiendo.*" I nod in sympathy. *I understand.*

The heavyset man asks where I'm from, then thrusts his chin at me and demands to know if I work back home.

"*Claro,*" I say. *Of course.*

His name is Carlos Espinosa Gasco. And once he gets warmed up, tucks in his shirt, and pushes back his errant wisps of hair, Carlos has a lot to say. Most of it is said so rapidly that I comprehend only snippets. But as he's gotten up a full head of steam, I see no point in slowing him down. Carlos just needs to talk. That I understand exactly what he's saying is unimportant, so long as I'm a receptive ear. And since his coffee is so good, it's easy for me. When I tell him that I must begin walking, he digs under the counter and comes up with a small, black-and-white laminated photo of a young boy. He presses it into my hand.

"Take it," he says. "That is me at five years old. I was a very happy child."

I go to refuse his offering, but his eyes tell me it is important to him. I smile at the photo of the round-faced boy wearing a baseball cap and put it in my pocket.

Back at the room, Sam is still asleep. Nothing of him is visible in bed, only a lump under the red bedspread. I've brought him a coffee. I'm aware that this is a mistake. Serving my son breakfast in bed, in essence rewarding his morning inertia, will only further entrench his sloth, and teach him nothing. On the other hand, my reasoning goes, it is in my interest that he get moving faster. Coffee might help that. It doesn't.

At 8:30, a half hour after our agreed departure time, I give him a last fifteen-minute warning. A hand comes out from under the covers, feels for the coffee cup, and brings it under the bedspread. A minute later, the hand reappears, putting the half-drunk coffee on the edge of the table. It falls to the floor, spilling the remains of the coffee.

"Shit," a rasping voice comes from under the covers.

After yesterday's fight, I am not looking for another. At 8:45, with no further sign of movement, I walk out the door.

The way out of Najera hugs the high red rocks that stand guard over the town. The clay path climbs, and in short order, long grass and then red rolling hills filled with vineyards dominate the vista. Occasional tractors work the fields and take no heed of a lone walker hurrying along under the morning sun. I cross the Río Valdecañas.

I enjoy my solitude while I miss Sam's company. It's during these early hours of walking each day that Sam is often most forthcoming, that I get a glimpse into what and how he's thinking, where his feelings lay. It's when he is usually most receptive. It is also when my mind is freshest, I'm at my most patient, and I feel the possibility of a new day. It's during these first few hours that we share an easy camaraderie that encourages ideas to flow back and forth. It's a time when feelings are most easily dissected, accepted, discarded—before the heat and distance traveled turn the day into a battle of attrition, when exhaustion makes tempers short and hunger or frustration squelch generosity of spirit. While I spend much of my life craving time alone, I fear that this—my setting out solo—will become the new norm on our walk.

Traveling on my own this morning, thinking in this way, I'm aware of the paradox that treading over a public landscape such as the open trail I'm on is in many ways a very private experience. I pass another sign for Guillermo's Taxi, this one on the side of an abandoned shed. I'm surprised to see another advertisement. It was so long ago and so far away when I saw the earlier sign yesterday, his territory must be huge, I conclude. Then I remember that all the hours I've walked since then are easily covered by a car in just a few minutes. Perspective.

Sam catches up with me outside the Café Sevilla in the village of Azofra. He's excited.

"I've been thinking about Finisterre."

"Yeah?"

"I mean, Santiago, what's that? I'm not a pilgrim. The story of Santiago means nothing to me."

"Fair enough," I say.

"Do it with me, Dad."

I've been thinking about Finisterre since Sam has been toying with the idea. I would love to march to the sea with my son—or more accurately, I would love to want to march to the sea with my son. But it feels right that Sam go on without me—and it feels righter still that I sit my already weary ass down for two days at the end of the journey.

"No, Sammy," I say, "Santiago will be enough for me. I'm not doing it for any religious reasons either, obviously. But Santiago is my goal, and that's where I'm stopping."

I was raised a Catholic and dragged to Mass by my mother each Sunday growing up, while my father attended church with us only on Christmas and Easter. Most grueling was the monthly "folk Mass," in which my brother Stephen played guitar. It wasn't the rousing versions of

"Kumbaya" and "Blowin' in the Wind" that I found so painful, but that the singing extended the forty-five minutes of agony to an hour.

I long ago walked away from the dogma of my religion, even as seeds of a spiritual connection to something beyond my comprehension began to grow in me. That I've raised my children without formal religion is something I don't regret, having chosen instead to speak to them openly and often of some form of belonging and universal meaning, encouraging their own search for such a connection. But I confess to occasionally wondering whether the absence of an active exposure to structured doctrine pertaining to the larger questions has left a void, or if it has allowed the space for personal probing that I find essential to real meaning.

"You think the Santiago story is meaningless?" I say, "Dig this."

"Is it more Camino history?"

"Sort of."

"I need a cigarette," Sam says, and rummages while I launch into the story of the "hanged innocent" of Santo Domingo de la Calzada, today's destination. Legend says that the son of a Germanic family passing through on pilgrimage caught the eye of a local girl. Being devout, he rejected her advances. Scorned, she planted pieces of silver in his bag. He was arrested and hanged. The young man's family, heartbroken, continued to Santiago in his honor. On the return trip, they stopped in Santo Domingo, discovered him still hanging from the tree and still alive, apparently kept that way by the saint as a reward for his devotion. The family rushed to the magistrate to explain the situation. Just sitting down to dinner, the magistrate bellowed, "That boy is no more alive than the chicken on this table before me." At which point the plucked and cooked bird rose from the plate and began to strut around, very much alive. To this day, live chickens are kept in a place of honor in the Cathedral in Santo Domingo.

"We'll see them tonight," I tell Sam.

Perhaps missing my point, he tells me of a video he saw on YouTube of a plucked chicken hopping around. "It was the most disgusting thing I ever saw."

Not to be outdone, I tell him about the goat I saw beheaded in Calcutta, how it kept bleating after being decapitated.

We march on—not as devout pilgrims perhaps, but a father and son making our way west over internal terrain.

As we do, Sam begins to sing the same line from Bob Dylan's "Hurricane" over and over and over and over. I regret exposing him to what was, until this moment, one of my favorite songs. He then pontificates on the merits and evils of TikTok.

"It really connects people. But it's a life suck. I deleted it this morning," he tells me.

"I thought you deleted it a few days ago."

"I did."

"I see."

"I downloaded it again."

"Yeah. I put that together."

"It's just very addictive."

"Apparently."

Then Sam makes the arbitrary declaration, "Once we get to the top of this hill, we'll have a whole new landscape. Let that be a lesson to you."

I really miss my earlier solitude.

At the rise of the next hill, we come upon the bizarre phantom urbanism of Cirueña. Never-occupied, early twenty-first century and now decaying apartment structures, paved cul-de-sacs with no houses, and perhaps most peculiar, a well-manicured golf course, were all someone's bad idea. A hundred people live in a town that was built for thousands who never showed up. Whereas all the villages, towns, and cities we have traveled through, no matter their intrinsic appeal, sprang organically over centuries from need, Cirueña was an arbitrary decision, and a failed one. Tattered, faded *Se Vende* signs are ubiquitous. The sky, brilliant blue for the past week, has turned dirty gray. The wind is blowing as it hasn't the entire time we've been in Spain, and there's a chill in the air not felt since the Pyrenees. We stop at the Rioja Alta Golf Club and have a Coke. To add to the surreal quality of the moment, Sam turns to me and asks, "How are you, Dad?" It's a genuine question he's posing. One I don't recall him asking me on the trip up to now. And he's looking for an answer.

I'm so taken off guard that I stammer in response. How am I? I'm preoccupied, watering weeds of habitual distress. I don't want my son to know how heavily I at times feel the weight of responsibility to provide, or how I misassign so many other anxieties onto money and that responsibility, and how that clouds my judgment. I've been thinking about my wife, my fear that I'm in some ways just not enough to handle the love that's been directed at me. I tell myself that Sam is my son and not a confidant with whom I share secret insecurities. I remember as a young child when my mother, on a few occasions, told me things that perhaps she shouldn't have—frustrations and disappointments. Were these just passing moods, unfounded late-night fears? Or were they convictions arrived at through bitter experience? Regardless, when put upon a child, they were interpreted as settled fact. But Sam is no longer a child. Maybe my reluctance is all bullshit, and I'm just scared to show my son who I am for fear he'll be disappointed. Then, disappointing myself and letting him down even as I open my mouth, I say, "I'm good, Sammy. Although I'm cold, which is weird, given that it's been so fucking hot."

When I last walked the Camino, most of the smaller towns and villages I passed along the way were in the midst of a centuries-long decline. The young had moved off to the cities, looking for opportunities and action. The streets were the domain of long-time widows, still dressed in black, often seen carrying brooms, sweeping off their tiny stoops. The resurgence of the Camino has brought the return of opportunity to many of these rural outposts, with populations increasing for the first time in decades. While Santo Domingo de la Calzada, with its six thousand plus residents, was always more prosperous than many of its neighboring towns, the industrial outskirts are a sign of more recent growth.

Unfortunately, the hotel I booked is closer to these fringes than the old medieval quarter I remember so well. Since it is run by Cistercian nuns, I wrongly assumed it would be near the twelfth-century cathedral in the center. The diminutive woman in the black-and-white habit is slow to respond to the bell at the front desk. When she appears, there are no words of greeting, nor any response to my queries on her well-being. Instead, she gets right down to business.

"You pay now," the nun says.

"Okay." I pull out my wallet. "Can I give you a credit card?"

"No."

"Oh. The sign there says you accept credit cards, and there's the machine." I point to both.

"Cash."

She still has not looked at me, instead busying herself by shuffling papers on the desk in front of her.

"Okay." I begin to count out the money. "Is it possible to get two keys?"

"No."

I look over at Sam. He's crouched down on his haunches, leaning against the wall, scrolling on his phone.

"And what time does breakfast start?" I ask.

"There's a bar down the street."

"I thought breakfast was included."

"No."

I put my money down on the counter.

"You leave by eleven." She reaches for the cash.

I beat her to it.

"I'll do you one better, Sister," I say. "I'll leave now."

"Maybe it affected my hardwire"

351 miles to Santiago

"I realized I blame my father for everything," Louisa says to me. We're sitting at an outdoor café off the Plaza Alameda. I'm waiting for a pizza I just ordered. The intense, attractive woman was passing by and recognized me as a fellow pilgrim. She stopped to say hello, took a seat, and started talking. My feet are throbbing, and I've still got to find us a place to sleep after my impulsive re-rejection of the Catholic Church.

I nod and consider her remark. There's very little blame left in me toward my own father—in fact, there never was much. But that I was terrified of him there is no doubt. Coming through the front door after being away on one of his not infrequent business trips, my father always shouted, "Hello! Hello! Hello!" in rising crescendo. On one occasion, my mother was tucking me into bed as his car turned in the driveway, the front door opened, and his salutation rang out.

"Come on, sweetie, you can get up and say hello to your father," my mother said as she rose from the side of my bed.

"Can you just say I was asleep?" I asked.

My mother quickly kissed my check and turned out the light.

But Louisa, leaning in toward me now, doesn't seem afraid of much—although she does seem a bit old to still be blaming it all on Daddy. Regardless, her forthcoming manner makes things easy on me. I just have to listen.

She's from Majorca. A podiatrist who recently quit her practice. "I was burnt out. It was too much pressure. So I gave it away, gave away all my money, too. I let it all go. Now I live the Buddha life."

Observing her, listening to her story without a word of prompting, she strikes me as either on the verge of a nervous breakdown or a great personal liberation. Either way, it's sexy to watch.

"And now, I just keep going"—she leans even further toward me, holding my eye—"doing what I feel." Louisa's hand reaches out, past that invisible boundary between us and deep into my space. Not sure exactly what is expected of me now, I'm suddenly almost nervous. At that instant, Louisa sees her friend across the square, jumps up, and is gone. Never to be seen again.

Sam arrives, after a reconnaissance and a call to one of his buds back home. "Who was that?"

"That was Louisa, from Majorca."

Ever the keen observer, Sam asks, "What'd she want?"

"I'm not entirely sure," I tell him honestly. "You find us a place to sleep?"

"No. Was I supposed to?"

The pizza arrives. We both dive in. It's terrible.

"There's a fancy place right next to the big church."

"I stayed there last time," I tell Sam. "I have a great memory of it. I was trying not to spoil you."

"Screw that, Dad. It looks great."

"You can hardly see them," Sam says, squinting at the glass-encased cage above the doorway near the back of the church, in which the straw-covered bottom all but obscures the fowl. "Your story about it was better."

And Sam is done with the Cathedral. We move on to the free-standing bell tower, across the square. Sam is irritable. The Ex has been texting him.

"She's messing with my head," he says as we climb flight after flight of the winding stone steps.

The moment we reach the top, the dozen or more bells begin to ring out the hour. It's a deafening, piercing clanging that goes on and on. If the inside of Sam's head sounds anything like this, the kid is suffering.

A good meal and vibrant street life provide relief and distraction. After Sam slips off to prowl the back lanes and talk with his friends at home, I come upon a street concert, complete with stage lights, a one-man band, and backup singer in a red sequined dress. They rock the locals with a Spanish rendition of "My Way," recognizable and equally crowd-pleasing in any language.

Back outside our swanky hotel—once a pilgrims' hospital—I sit in the Plaza del Santo, the cathedral to my left. The late-evening sky turns from cobalt blue to black over the bell tower in front of me. The meticulously inlaid town square and surrounding stone buildings are awash in golden light. While many of the memories from my first Camino have faded or morphed, this place is precisely how I remember it. Sam strolls up. Before he speaks, I can see that he's relaxed; his edge for now is gone. He sits beside me. A warm breeze blows. Sam launches into a story about one of his friend's follies back home, and we laugh.

"Rocco's a fool, Sammy."

"I know. I love him."

The dramas of the day are behind; tomorrow is not a worry yet. I've wanted to get back to this exact spot for twenty-six years, but I never imagined it with my son beside me. Sometimes life is sweet.

"The Real Slim Shady" is barking out at me. My café con leche is smooth this morning, and I'm tempted to drop a coin in the El Dorado slot machine under the TV blaring Eminem. Sam goes to order us another coffee as an American woman makes her way over to him at the bar. She's from New York. She heard us speaking English. Her twenty-three-year-old son comes up behind her. He's smiling. I don't recognize them at all.

Their story is difficult to track, but it seems they had trouble finding a place to sleep. So they took a cab last night from somewhere (I couldn't catch where) to get here. The woman had what she describes as a "meltdown."

"So I think we're tapping out today," she says. "I can't not know where we're going to sleep."

I mention a helpful website and offer to write it down.

"But when I call no one answers!"

"Just book online, click the 'book' tab," I suggest.

She's really worked up and not hearing me.

"We're tapping out, we're tapping out," she just keeps repeating.

I'm slow to understand exactly what this means.

Sam steps up. "Don't do that. Just walk one more day. It'll get better." He puts his hand on her shoulder, trying to settle the woman. He's looking to reason with her son. "Really, just another day. It's just walking. Just keep going."

I step back and watch my son.

"Maybe. Maybe," she says.

"Trust me, it'll get better," Sam says. "Don't quit."

"Well, maybe."

But then that won't do. They're tapping out. They're really happy they met us. It'll help them next time. But they're tapping out.

It's almost 11:00 a.m., and we need to start walking.

The trail today is largely on a dirt track directly beside the N-120 highway. There is no shade. Fields of wheat stretch to the horizon. Sam keeps glancing back, keeping an eye out for the mother and son, hoping they decided to keep walking. Far behind us, just crossing the bridge out of town, two small figures appear.

"Think that's them?" Sam asks.

I turn and look, squinting into the sun. "Can't tell," I say.

We walk and talk again about my divorce from Sam's mother. He concludes, "I mean, maybe it's affected my hardwire, but it didn't upset me in an active, conscious way."

I'm reminded of a moment when Sam was still a very young child, a moment I've never forgotten. One I think will always haunt me. Coming into my bedroom early on a Sunday morning, Sam saw my now wife, his stepmother, in my bed for the first time. He turned and went racing from the room, crying, calling out, "Nooooo!" as he ran. Oh, how we hurt those we love.

Sam looks back again. The two distant people are still walking up the trail, too far behind for us to see clearly.

"Who are those guys?" Sam asks.

The way he asks the question reminds me of the movie *Butch Cassidy and the Sundance Kid*. The outlaws are on the run and being pursued by a relentless posse. More than once, Redford and Newman look over their shoulders, then one icon or the other asks that same question, in the same way that Sam just did.

I relay this story to Sam. It seems to me that he couldn't really care less.

"It's a really famous line." I try to impress my point upon him.

"No, I get it. I get it. It's a good story."

"Oh my God, please don't pity me."

A car horn blares. We turn toward the highway beside us and see a white taxi. The mother and her son are in the back seat. They are waving wildly out the window to us as they pass, apparently on their way to the airport in Burgos, tapping out.

We sit on a bench outside the San Lazaro bar. Five men—four with bellies and one rail thin—sit around a table, drinking beer under an umbrella, protected from the noon sun. A dozen pigeons circle the bell tower of the small church across the narrow street. They land in the belfry, then decide to repeat the exercise. Sam has made an equally momentous decision.

"Bro, from now on I'm switching to café negro. Milk in coffee is for wimps."

"You gonna start smoking Marlboros too?"

"No, they're gross."

Back out among the wheat, and corn, and suddenly endless fields of sunflowers, Sam explains to me the concept of 'love bombing,' then goes on about A.I. and then narcissism.

"I mean, I think I have a slightly narcissistic personality," he confesses.

"I think that's called being a teenager."

"Yo, I'm almost twenty."

"You know you're still young when you make a point of how *old* you are," I say.

"But like, I'm pretty obsessed with myself." Despite his self-flagellating words, Sam's mood is carefree.

"Again, that's being a teenager," I say. And despite my easy dismissals, I'm not feeling so blithe.

I've got a low, not quite identifiable agitation simmering. I noticed it as I was walking out the door this morning. The root cause remains just out of my reach. These damn sunflowers don't help. I've always found sunflowers a disturbing, almost sinister flower. And to make things worse, someone has plucked out seeds from the center of a few of them to create grinning, mocking faces.

Sam becomes fixated on his phone.

Looking to vent some of my floating frustration, I snap, "What are you doing?"

"I'm looking at the map," Sam says. His Snapchat is open. "See, we're pretty far along." Sam's little green man is bopping down the trail, a third of the way across Spain. "We'll make it. To Santiago."

And then I realize what's got me agitated. I had been glancing at the map in my book over breakfast and for a moment thought of just how far we have yet to travel. "There's still so much to overcome, so much can still happen," I remember thinking with dread. "How will we ever make it?"

I smile at Sam—fretful age acknowledging confident youth. I put my arm around his shoulder.

"I love that little green Snapchat man."

Sam grimaces. "Dude, you're all sweaty."

"Literally, I'd like to be finished"

337 miles to Santiago

The next morning we're grinding our way out of Belorado, a hardscrabble town with a make-no-apologies charm, in the steep valley of the Río Tirón. Sam was down last night. Before he left for Spain, he and The Ex had agreed to speak on yesterday's date. They didn't. Out in the street, under the light in front of our lodging, Sam could be heard on the phone with members of his posse back home late into the night, talking, listening, ranting, sometimes laughing. Today his mood is still clouded, but we walk on—always on the Camino, we walk on. We pass in and out of villages clinging to life by the thinnest of margins. By 11:00 a.m., the heat is stultifying.

In the hamlet of Tosantos there are no services, no fountain to fill our water bottles, no people to be seen. We sit on the only bench in the sliver of shade provided by the bolted church. A lone bird, a vulture, glides slowly over.

"Literally," Sam says, "I'd like to be finished with this walk."

I take the comment personally but show nothing. "There's not a lot of glamour at the moment."

We sit and sweat. We finish the water in our bottles.

"All you can do is walk through it, Sam," I say.

He knows I am only partially talking about this trudge we are on today.

"Come on, let's keep going."

Sam pushes himself up. "I'm gonna grow a mullet," he declares.

"Maybe you should just lie down here in the sun and let the vultures pluck your eyes out, instead."

In Espinosa del Camino, the streets are deserted save for a stout old woman wearing an apron over a floral dress. She stands, holding a broom, taking a break from sweeping up outside a small house with a row of colored beads hanging from the open door.

"*Hola!*" I call out as we pass.

The old woman nods gravely. "*Un abrazo por el Santo,*" she sings out.

"*Si, claro. Gracias.*" I nod back.

"What did she say?" Sam asks.

"A hug for the Saint," I translate. "It's what you used to hear on the trail, before people started saying '*Buen Camino.*'" I go on, answering his unasked question. "Behind the altar in the Cathedral in Santiago, there's a statue of Saint James. It's tradition that when you arrive, you embrace the statue, giving thanks to the saint for watching over you on your walk, and a blessing for all the people who helped you along the way."

"That's cool." Sam shrugs.

"It is," I assure him. "It was actually a very powerful experience the last time. I could feel my heart pounding against the statue when I hugged it. I started to cry."

"Well," Sam says. "I mean, let's face it. That's not much of an ask, Dad."

It's true. I am an easy cry. I've been known to shed tears at a good karate chop by my kids in martial arts classes.

Ahead, in Villafranca Montes de Oca, we at last find some lunch— a sandwich of egg and tomato and tuna fish. It's mouthwatering—and something that under normal circumstances might disgust me. The climb out of town, up, across, and over, and up again and over the Oca mountains, catches me unaware. The sprawling vistas we've been walking over these past days are gone. A dirt track, flanked in places by purple wildflowers, rises through a forest of oak and then dense pine. At first there is welcome shade; then the trail widens into a dirt road, and the surrounding forest can offer no protection from the sun overhead. Although utterly unpopulated, The Way now feels oddly claustrophobic. I have the paranoid thought that people might be watching from the trees. Only at the end of the day's walk will I learn that, centuries ago, pilgrims were terrified walking through these mountains, so liable were they to be robbed by bandits.

I'm still irritated at Sam for saying he wished the Camino were over. He was upset about not speaking with The Ex yesterday. I understand. That he's misplacing his frustrations on the Camino is normal. Like any meaningful relationship, this walk acts as a receptacle for our fears, doubts, and resentments, while summoning our more noble traits. It tests our patience and endurance, while offering up satisfaction, moments of delight, and bone deep intimacy. Regardless, I'm relieved when he marches ahead as we leave Villafranca. Powering up the hill, I can hear him singing away his sorrows until the trees and distance swallow him.

Last night, his friend suggested he listen to Hemingway's *The Old Man and the Sea*. "It'll change your life," his friend promised. I hadn't read it in years, so we agreed to each listen hiking over the mountains today.

Donald Sutherland purrs in my ears. He hooks the big fish, and a lizard darts across the trail in front of me. A hot wind blows across the sweat on my arms. The fish drags the old man farther out to sea. A cloud passes over the sun. I whisper, "Thank you," without looking up. The fish finally jumps. I sit and rest on a stump. He lashes the fish to the boat. I trudge on. The sharks attack as white and yellow butterflies flutter in front of me. At last, the trail descends. The old man finally sleeps.

San Juan de Ortega has one church, two cafés, no shops, and a population—depending on whom you speak to—of twenty to thirty. It also exerts a powerful pull. At Bar Marcela, Sam gets his daily hit of ice cream—each town along the way seems to have the exact same freezer filled with the exact same selection of ice cream. Sam has three he likes and rotates depending on mood. I order an omelet, chat for a few minutes with the man at the bar, then take a seat outside to wait. As I look over at the church, my feet up on the plastic chair opposite me, the heat is sharp. The umbrella helps only a little.

"My Spanish is actually coming along," I say to Sam, who is leaning forward, elbows on his knees, concentrating on his ice cream.

"Yeah?" he says, paying me no attention.

"No, seriously," I say. "I mean, I was just talking with the guy who owns this place. He was going on about how there are fewer pilgrims this year, talking about the other café here and all this other stuff. I was totally following everything he was saying with ease."

Sam is down to his final few bites, his head tilted at an angle, licking the melting cone. "He was speaking English."

"What?"

Sam looks at me. "Are you joking?"

"What do you mean?"

"That guy, the guy who took your order, he was speaking English."

I blink a few times. "Really?"

"I'm gonna get a Coke. You want one?"

"I better, yeah."

It really is hot.

Sam returns with the Cokes, and the owner brings out my omelet.

"Thank you," I say in English.

"You're welcome, my friend," he says in English.

An hour with my feet up the wall and my head is clearer. I go and sit on top of a picnic table across from the church, under a small tree. The complete absence of any diversion here, the palpable stillness of the place, has the effect of making me feel as if I'm being swaddled, or held firmly in the hand of something. I wonder how long I could stay here before the need to move out into the world again overtook me.

Sam strolls up. "Bored?" I ask.

He sticks out his lower lip and shakes his head. "No. I thought this place was a shithole at first, but it's actually pretty cool."

As the heat has begun to lose some of its intensity, the swallows have started to dart around the eaves of the church. We head over to the other café and have pizza for dinner.

"How'd you like *The Old Man and the Sea*?" I ask.

"I mean"—he scrunches his face—"it was good."

"Didn't change your life?"

The man beside us at dinner is from Toronto. His name is Scott. He's walking the Camino because he "needed to do something."

Scott is also jumping in a car in the morning. "I misjudged how much time it would take, so I'm gonna skip the Meseta and go on to León and keep going from there."

"You're going to skip the Meseta?' I ask. "Probably smart." The Meseta is the high plain after the city of Burgos, which we will arrive in tomorrow. It is barren, hot, desolate, in many ways the most challenging part of the walk.

After Scott leaves, Sam turns to me. "What's with all these people taking cabs? I mean, why bother to come at all?"

"Walk your own Camino, dude. But yeah, I know what you mean."

"Why'd you tell him he was smart to skip the Meseta? You said it was the most amazing part."

"I said it was the most intense part. And you're right, I wouldn't miss it."

"So?"

I shrug. "I've got no stake in him. I'm not here to make him feel bad."

"But seriously, how hard is it to look at the calendar and then look at the book and figure out how many days it takes? It says it right there."

"We all justify what we need to justify," I say.

The sun has finally set, and the sky is turning. A swallow races past my head so fast and so close that I feel a brush of wind in the otherwise still air. The birds are diving, swooping. Mostly they play around the church. With such movement occupying the periphery of the stillness surrounding us, silence is easy to endure. We wander off, no destination in mind.

Sam mentions The Ex.

"We all try to get the other person to change to meet our desires of how they should behave," I tell him. "It's a guaranteed ticket to frustration."

"Yeah," he mumbles.

"Just ride the roller coaster, Sammy."

He turns away from me and drifts off toward the dying light, down the middle of the only road leading out of town. We've seen no cars come or go since our arrival several hours earlier. After a few hundred yards, Sam stops and sits down cross-legged in the middle of the pavement. The sky is turning purple. Places like San Juan de Ortega can kick up a lot—there's nowhere to hide. I stand far back and watch Sam gazing off, the night coming on around him.

Part 2

We ourselves must walk the path.

—*Buddha*

"You must be young and stupid"

322 miles to Santiago

The day starts badly. The TV in El Descanso Café is on. I'm watching Neil Diamond sing something called "If There Were No Dreams," and like passing a seven-car pile-up on the highway, I can't look away. I guzzle my café con leche and hurry down my eggs, grab a black coffee for Sam, and head back outside. Here, at least, there is silence. The air is cool and moist. The sun can just be made out over the trees, a dim and out of focus orb seen through the thick gauze of fog that fills the valley. The sun will have its way with the day, but not yet. The swallows that played with so much vigor on the west side of the church at sunset now celebrate the morning on the east side—whether I or anyone else are here to see it.

My reverie is interrupted by an open-faced American. His name is Duncan. He's from Oregon. He clearly wants to chat—but I just barely survived Neil Diamond.

"*Buen Camino*," he gushes as I start away.

"*Buen Camino*," I mutter over my shoulder, hurrying up the walk and trying not to spill my son's coffee.

My wife accuses me of becoming a misanthrope—it has basis in fact.

"It really is rough without sugar," Sam says from under the covers, managing to place the coffee back on the bedside table without incident. His voice is thick with sleep. I pack my toiletries.

"You can grab a café con leche on the way out, if you want."

"No, Dad. You don't get it. Real men drink it black." When Sam announced to the world that he was becoming a black coffee drinker a

101

few days earlier, moving on from café con leche and leaving his Monster energy drinks behind like childhood, one of his friends sent him a You-Tube video on how to get used to drinking black coffee. Sam offers to show it to me. I decline the invitation.

"Not man enough, Dad?"

"That's it exactly, Sam."

The air still has its welcome—if fleeting—chill, and the fog is soft against the skin as we leave the tarmac and join a dirt trail. The walk today will lead us to the city of Burgos, with a population of more than 175,000. I glance back for a last look, but after just steps, tiny San Juan is gone from view and part of our past.

Sam seems to have turned some kind of corner regarding his relationship with The Ex this morning. "I stayed in this thing longer than I should have," he acknowledges for the first time. We're through scrubland and pine, then open pasture. "People always say they left a relationship long after they should have. I get that now."

We pass the village of Agés and cross the Río Vena over a stone bridge. The sun has burned away the fog. Then we're road walking, which I find uninspiring at best and often discouraging, even dangerous. Sharing the way with cars and trucks has a draining effect on me, while Sam is undeterred by such facts of life, his only problem being he tends to drift away from the edge of the road toward its center.

"Sam, stay on the side of the road, please."

"Whatever."

And we're back to our parent/twelve-year-old-child dynamic.

With his mind still on relationships, Sam tackles marriage. "I'm not sure how logical marriage is. I mean, it's about a fifty percent success rate. Then you consider that most of the people that stay married are unhappy. The odds are not good."

"True. But..." When it's all said and done, I believe in love, its challenges and sacrifices and joys and rewards. "It's the only game in town."

"I can tell you this," Sam says. "I'm definitely getting married on the downward slope."

"Meaning?"

"You can't tell what I mean by that?"

"You mean when you're older? After you've messed around all you want and squeezed all the joy out of life?"

"Exactly."

"Wow, that's going to be one lucky girl."

"Hey, you must be young and stupid before you can be old and wise."

"That's very wise, Sam."

We leave the pavement and begin to climb Sierra Atapuerca on a gradual slope over terrain scattered with rock, scrub trees, and occasional rows of planted pines. Fog rolls in again. Old and tangled barbed wire lines one side of an ill-defined trail over the long crest of the climb. Windmills, looking as if their blades will never move, sit on the horizon to the north. A low humming sound seems to rise from the earth. Our conversation has strung itself out amid long silences of walking both together and apart. Each time we pick up as if there has been no pause.

"When are we adults?" Sam asks.

"That's a good question," I say. And one for which I have no ready answer.

"I used to think it was when I turned twenty-one," Sam continues.

"The only thing I can tell you for sure is that it ain't on the day you turn twenty-one."

"I know, but like..." He shrugs.

"It's a process, I suppose. An incremental thing." Then I attempt the old joke—"I'll let you know when it happens to me."

But like it or not, I am an adult. And that happened at 9:32 p.m. on March 15, 2002.

My eldest son was born blue and unresponsive. His Apgar score—the test given moments after birth and measuring initial signs of health—was zero out of ten. The room flooded with doctors. Orders were barked out. Monitors began to sound. My body began jumping up and down without my consent. "No. No," I kept saying. In time, a faint gasp of breath led to a small cry. Traces of color came into Sam's skin. While much of the attending medical staff drifted off, several others continued to huddle over Sam and prod and manipulate him.

Then, as they relaxed in their work, they began to speak of another baby on the unit. I saw myself step forward and heard myself say, with a force I didn't know I possessed, "This is the most important baby in this hospital." Shamed, one doctor said, "You're absolutely right, sir."

The city of Burgos comes into distant view in the valley below. Tracing the path back from the spire of its cathedral, I can see the slanting rooftops of the old center, the long industrial outskirts, the airport, and the villages and fields of wheat and sunflowers we must pass through. All threaded with highways, roads, and lanes.

"God, that's a long way," I say. But at least the humming sound has been explained. An ugly strip mine to the north is kicking up a cloud of white dust high into the air.

In the village of Villaval we get turned around, passing a pair of pilgrims going one direction, then a few minutes later, we pass them again going in the other. In Cardeñuela Riopico, I tend to what is somehow just my first blister of the Camino. Duncan, the bearded puppy-dog of a pilgrim I met this morning in San Juan, approaches and asks if his fiancée, Hallie, who has seen me in some movies, can take a photo. She wants to re-create the poster pose from a silly movie called *Weekend at Bernie's*, in which a dead man (Bernie) is held up by two fools (one of which was me). For some reason, this is a not uncommon request, but one that takes me off guard here on the Camino. While Hallie plays "dead," Duncan and I flank her and smile. Sam takes the photo.

Walking out of town, Sam is preoccupied.

"What is it?" I break the silence.

He considers and then finally speaks. "They were the whitest people I have ever met."

Sam puts in his earbuds, and we troop on, walking along the edge of the pavement. Charged by music, Sam begins to stride ahead, then begins to drift farther into the road. I've started to grow increasingly worried about Sam's tendency to wander into the middle of active roads. I call to him to move over. With his music playing, he can't hear me. It's a small town and few cars have passed, but all the same, I call him again. He still can't hear me. I hustle to catch up with him. From a few feet behind, I tell him again to move over. He's still unresponsive. I reach out with my walking stick to tap him on the side of the shoulder, as if I were directing cattle. My frustration is greater than I realize, and my stick smacks on his scallop shell attached to the side of his pack. I hear a loud crack and several small pieces of the shell break off and fall to the ground. Sam has not noticed but turns at the feel of the rap.

"Move. Over," I tell him.

He complies without comment.

The obvious metaphorical significance of this act is not lost on me— in the name of protecting the child, frustrated parent lashes out and does more harm than good.

As the traditional Camino here is long paved under, there are several options on how to get into the city. Just beyond the underpass of the A-1 national highway, two women are standing at a crossroads, consulting their map. One path is along the highway all the way in—an ugly, loud, and potentially unsafe few hours of walking. The other option loops around the airport, leading to a more pleasant experience through a park along the banks of the Río Arlanzón. This second option adds more than a mile to the day's walk.

Sam goes directly to the bottom line.

"Which one is longer?"

"They're the same," I lie.

"Just tell me. It's fine to go the other way, but just tell me."

"It's just better this way; the other way it too dangerous," I say, and turn away from the highway. "Come on."

"Fine, but it's obviously longer."

"Whatever. I'm going this way. It's too hot for this discussion."

Off the mountain and down here in the valley, there is no breeze. The sun is searing. Sam charges ahead, and I can hear him shouting, swearing along to his rap music. Dancing, he jumps left and right. Planes take off and land. The hour it takes to walk the wide, dusty road beside the barbed-wire-topped chain-linked fence that skirts the entire airport, past the factory spewing smoke, past the scrap yard, is not an hour that will appear in any brochure about the fabled Camino de Santiago.

At the edge of the N-120 four-lane highway, The Way diverges again. One option is well marked, running along the side of this less-intense-but-still-major road all the way to the center; the other option, and the one for which we endured the airport path, is across the highway and through a park leading to the riverside walk. It is less well marked, but according to my guidebook, easy enough to find and follow.

Since Sam was well ahead of me, he saw the obvious trail beside the highway and began down it. I cross over the highway and split my focus, trying to get Sam's attention while simultaneously attempting to find the less-well-marked trail to the river. Sam finally hears me calling him across the traffic. I wave him over. He insists he is on the trail. He points to a large sign, proving his point. I scream across traffic that I know, but he needs to cross over and follow me. Unaware of the riverside walk option (even though I told him), he insists I am wrong. I insist he follow. We continue this shouting match across the highway as traffic roars past, all the while walking toward the city. Eventually he acquiesces to my demands and crosses over, narrowly avoiding getting killed in the process. We are well down the road from where we should have slipped into the park to find the river. We double back, but I can't find the trail. We search. I ask a roadworks crew if they know where to find the Camino. In unison, they all point across the highway to the trail Sam was on. I tell them no, there is another trail, by the river. They look confused and point back to across the highway. No, I insist. The riverside walk. They turn their backs on me and resume working. I continue to search and then finally give up. We cross back over and begin to march down the trail by the highway that Sam was on. I apologize for messing us up, explaining how I had hoped for a nicer walk. "It's fine," he says, and means it. And we walk on. Minutes later, I look across the highway and see what appears to be a path heading into the woods. I insist we try again. Sam groans but follows. The path is a dead end. Instead of turning back, I press on, getting us lost in a deserted housing estate. This is not the way. I insist on looking around one more corner. Sam says he will wait for me and sits down on the curb. I get lost. I can't find him. Frantic phone calls follow. I accuse him of moving. He insists he has not budged. Eventually, Sam locates me and leads us back across the highway to the path he was on initially, and we trudge toward town by the side of the busy road. I am discouraged, humiliated, and tired.

"I'm sorry, Sam."

"Don't worry about it, Dad." He has all but forgotten the entire escapade and chats away amiably, discussing how he has already found a gym to go to.

"Your ability to let things go will serve you well, Sammy. Especially in this relationship."

"Whatever. You think they'll have sushi in Burgos?"

I'm starving, not to mention dehydrated and disoriented. My blister hurts. I am struggling more than I have up to this point. We pass a bakery. I go inside, and when I come back out gnawing on a *Napolitana de chocolate*, Sam is staring at the side of his backpack.

"Look, it's broken," he says, pointing to the chipped scallop shell. I'm about to admit my guilt in the matter when Sam says, "It's kind of cool.

I like it. As long as it doesn't break more." He hoists his pack and moves on. I swallow my guilt by finishing my pastry.

"I thought you weren't getting those anymore," Sam says, while we wait on a red light.

"Shut up."

Standing over a garbage can on the corner, I eat a second pastry, and regret not buying a third.

"All we're doing is walking"

306 miles to Santiago

Stomping ground of the medieval warlord El Cid, as well as the early seat of General Francisco Franco's government, the city of Burgos, often called the Gothic capital of Spain, is a formidable place. Most of the interest for a pilgrim is centered in the area around the twelfth-century cathedral. Most of Sam's interest is in eating sushi. Taking a seat at a table outside in the bustling Plaza de la Flora, the spires of the Cathedral are visible over Sam's shoulder. Being a city kid, he's been comfortable navigating along the narrow streets of the old town while I've had my feet up the wall, trying to get myself sorted out.

"I give this sushi a five out of ten," Sam says. "I mean, they just kind of squirted mayonnaise on top and called it spicy tuna. But I'll take it."

When we go off in search of ice cream, I reemphasize to Sam that we need to get an early start in the morning. "You think it's been hot up to now—there's a heat wave starting tomorrow, and the Meseta is very intense."

"Like how hot?"

"Like over a hundred degrees. There's no shade out there. We have to get going early."

"I gotcha," Sam says. "No problem."

The Meseta is a high plateau in northern Spain. There are few trees, fields of wheat and grain to the horizon in all directions, and only intermittent small villages with few services. The sky is vast. This goes on for several days and has been known to mess with the pilgrim's brain chemistry. Don Quixote wandered around the southern Meseta, and it explains a lot of his behavior. It was in the Meseta last trip that I suffered an unannounced sobbing meltdown in a field of wheat under midday sun. I've been afraid of the place ever since.

At 6:30 in the morning the Bo Diddly beat pours out of the small café, and a cool breeze blows down Calle Fernán Gonzáles. The spires of the cathedral are visible overhead in the predawn mist. Pilgrims are already walking. I eat in a hurry and, grabbing a black coffee to go, hustle back to rouse Sam. By 7:30 we're out the door. This is our earliest start of the Camino—by hours.

Sam needs another coffee if he is going to survive. We stop at the same café. Crosby, Stills, Nash & Young are playing at high volume. Sam goes in as I watch through the window. I'm impatient, anxious about the Meseta. I want to get going. Sam knows this. Coffee in a paper cup is placed down in front of him, he pays, then leans against the counter, consulting his phone. I watch through the window. He scrolls. I wait. He sips, blows on the coffee and sips again. I begin to fume. He continues to scroll.

Knowing I will be forgoing what is always the best part of our walk together if I leave, I struggle to hang on. Another part of me doesn't want to be servile, loitering here. My anxiety over the day ahead is growing. I take one last look through the window at my son consulting his phone and holding his coffee aloft without a care in the world. I leave.

Since we're on the road so early, there are a dozen disparate walkers forming a loose, strung-out pod on the way out of town. Before the old pilgrims' hospital by Universidad de Burgos, a Belgian physiotherapist, her face handsomely lined with the accumulation of thought and worry over the years, falls into step with me. Her name is Theresa. Theresa proves amiable company, until she begins to press me on my motives for walking the Camino. This kind of pilgrim probing is not uncommon, yet I always find such muscled intimacy off-putting. My habitual reply of

"I'm just walking" is generally regarded as the evasion it is. (But perhaps there is a larger truth in this simple statement.)

I can see that Theresa is now ready to give up on me, but because we are walking stride for stride, we are stuck together for the time being. "Is this your first Camino?" she asks, filling space.

When I tell her that I did it twenty-five years earlier, Theresa's opinion seems to shift, and she regards me now as a more interesting creature, someone perhaps worthy of her investment after all. This is when she confides that her nearly two weeks of walking has taught her to "release her expectations."

I can now hear Sam just a few hundred yards behind us, talking on the phone to one of his friends back home.

"Yeah, bro. Bro…"

Theresa will be leaving the Camino early, to get back to work. She will return at some future date to finish. This is something to which I cannot relate. Were I in a similar position, I'd start later in the Camino or not walk at all. The one thing I know for certain is that I would not begin something like this knowing I would not finish.

The loose group we're absently tracking suddenly stops. The lead person made a wrong turn. We backtrack a block and correct course. I hate being a sheep.

"So you live in New York," Theresa says. She tells me about the conferences she attends in Boulder, Colorado, how she'd love to visit New York, and I become aware that I can't hear Sam anymore. Looking back, I don't see him. The walk out of any city can be tricky, as the way is less well marked and distractions abound. The early-morning mist doesn't help.

I call him on the phone. It goes to voice mail. I call again.

"Yo, I'm on a call," he snaps. "What's up?"

"You made a wrong turn. Go back to the beginning of the park and make a right."

"Oh." His tone softens. "Thanks, bro."

I tell Theresa that I need to wait for my son.

"You're not alone?"

I smile and she walks on.

For the first time on the Camino, I feel ragged this morning. Always tired at the end of each day's walk, today I'm concerned for myself. I'm slightly quivery. For someone who made their career on being young, bordering old without ever passing through the middle is startling.

Sam catches up with me.

"Thanks, Dad."

"That's why I'm here, Sammy."

It takes more than an hour to come upon the first scraggly wheat field, under buzzing electrical wires ("You hear that, Dad?") beside a small housing project on the outskirts of the city. By nine o'clock the sun has burned through. By ten, the heat of the day is pressing down.

We pass through a nasty village and then a sweet-looking one. Then we are walking again on earth at last. There are no clouds in the sky. To the north, wind turbines stand with rigor mortis. Bales dry in the field beside us. Gnats begin to swarm in front of our faces. We swat at them foolishly. After another hour we crest a small rise and there it is— nothing. The Meseta proper lays itself out in front of us. Stalks of sun-scarred wheat to the horizon in three directions. We drop our packs, eat a peach, wipe on some sunscreen, and walk.

In the village of Hornillos del Camino, we sit in the gutter eating watermelon outside the lone shop. A pilgrim dressed in a long dark cloak, wearing a small-brimmed straw hat with a feather rising at a jaunty angle, carrying an embroidered bag across his chest, props his long walking stick against the closest wall and sits in the gutter a few feet away.

"*Muy caliente.*" He smiles at me, using the incorrect Spanish expression for hot.

"Very," I say in return.

He has a round face, covered in an unkempt beard, and is wearing small round glasses that do nothing to hide a wicked gleam in his eye. This is James. An Englishman living in a small coastal village in the west of Ireland, he is walking his twentieth Camino.

"Twenty?" Sam is incredulous.

James nods. "I usually do it twice a year."

Something in James reminds me of another Camino character named Vitorino, whom I encountered just up the road in Hontanas, on my first trip. Bewildered from the sun, I stumbled into a dark bar for a Coke during the heat of the day. A small man with a flat nose came and sat beside me. He held a pitcher of red wine in his knarled hand. Without a word, Vitorino lifted the jug and poured it on his third eye in the middle of his forehead; the wine cascaded directly down between his eyebrows, along the bridge of his nose, made a small ski jump, and landed on his outstretched tongue. I watched him drink the entire pitcher in one go and wondered if I was hallucinating.

While admitting to no party tricks himself, James does confess to liking "a bottle of red wine in the evening and a good snore. Which is why I usually sleep out. I don't want to be public enemy number one."

"You sleep outside?" Sam asks. "Where?"

James shrugs. "There are a lot of good places. The next town has a lovely portico in front of the church."

Feeling like amateurs, Sam and I hoist our packs and continue. Grinding through the heat, I mutter, "It's intense, isn't it?"

Sam, who seems as fresh as if he's just had an invigorating dip in a cool stream, shrugs. "All we're doing is walking, mate."

The Australian accent is back.

"Oh, no. Please, Sam. No. Stop."

"Well, mate, come on, now. We'll throw some shrimp on the barbie when we get in."

I try to ignore him. "God, it's hot."

But Sam is on a roll. "Maybe for a beta male, mate."

Sam is more comfortable with his own sense of masculine identity than I felt with mine in youth. Shadows of my discomfort have lingered into middle life. But watching my feet kick up dust as I walk, I question whether I really do still harbor such insecurities, as I habitually claim, or are they, like a worn-out shirt, a thing I wear out of habit. As a child, and for so long after, I associated manhood with my father's anger and explosiveness—even after the proof of my own experience told me that didn't need to be the case. I used that youthful perception equating manhood with volatility to safeguard against such explosiveness, but that censoring suppressed other areas of expression and keep me, at least to some degree, from fully inhabiting my place in the world.

"Come on, mate," Sam barks out. "You're draggin' your feet."

I knew I was afraid of the Meseta for a reason.

"I'm not gonna do this now"

286 miles to Santiago

A single yellow butterfly appears close in front of me, flitting. We travel together, and then my focus shifts through to the deep distance just in time to see Sam disappearing on the horizon. I watch him slip down into the earth, and when I return my gaze back, the butterfly is gone. Sweat is pouring from my body. It is well over a hundred degrees. A dozen wind turbines are just over the horizon to my right. I can see only the upper reaches of their dormant blades, stretching up into the sky like a plea. Beyond, the Cantabrian Mountains are a faded sketch in the afternoon haze.

I begin moving with great purpose. Breathing deeply, rhythmically. The Allman Brothers Band is playing in my headphones, loud. As Duane and Greg trade licks, I'm flying down the trail, my fingers air guitar/pianoing along. In high school, I used to listen to this music in the car while my older brother Peter drove us home from whatever Friday night party it was that I got drunk at. I haven't heard it in years. What a feeling it must have been for the two brothers to create such music together. I think of my own brothers. My family disintegrated when my mother left my father as I went off to college, and my early fame blew up the well-established dynamic between my brothers and me—from which it never fully recovered. I stride over the dirt track, and it strikes me in a moment of clear-eyed sentiment that this is perhaps my greatest regret.

My father also had three brothers (and a sister). I never understood if they were close in any real way. I saw only one of the brothers more than rarely—he had a deep scar running through one eye and he frightened me as a small child. My own brother told me a story that was revealing and helped me to understand the family dynamic in which my father was raised. When my father's mother, my grandmother, was very old, she was placed in a nursing home. Soon after her admittance, my father went to visit her and, in essence, kidnapped her, taking her to a motel. It was clear he didn't have a plan but was motivated by some need to act. The following day, my father's eldest brother came and confronted my father. The two firmly middle-aged men stood in the motel parking lot arguing, when suddenly my uncle hauled off and smacked my father hard up the side of his head. My father, the youngest sibling, just stood and received the abuse.

On hearing this story, my heart broke for my dad.

Sam's relationships with his own siblings are far different—and distinctly Sam. Two stories best illustrate. When Sam's sister, Willow—nearly five years younger and born of a different mother—performed on Broadway in a musical at eight years old, Sam was almost preternaturally cool on opening night. (I nearly had a stroke, while Dolores was her expansive self.) "She did really well," Sam concluded after the show. When we went backstage to congratulate Willow, Sam raced ahead and threw his arms around his sister and wouldn't let go. He wept in a way I had never witnessed in him, his pride for her taking us all by surprise. On another occasion, when Sam's younger brother by eleven years, Rowan, first understood that they had different mothers, he approached Sam and said, "We're only half brothers, Sam." Sam, who appeared to have been paying little attention, stopped, got to his knees, and took hold of his sibling's shoulders, looking him directly in the eyes, and said softly and without equivocation, "We're brothers, Rowan." There has never been a discussion on the matter since.

At ten in the evening, it is still ninety-three degrees. A silver slipper of a moon rises in a darkening sky. The herky-jerky movement of bats is visible around the belfry of La Iglesia de Nuestra Señora de la Inmaculada Concepción. Slid into a crease of the Meseta, Hontanas, with a population of just seventy, has the feeling of being a protected and private enclave.

I sleep well and set out by 6:30 the following morning. Sam, concluding that I had grossly overstated the perils of the Meseta, has decided that today he will get up when he rises and walk alone.

The temperature will climb nearly fifty degrees today, but now the air is cool. The road is deserted, the sun not yet over the horizon. A distant dog barks. A rooster crows, and I'm reminded of our third morning when the rooster woke Sam in Zubiri. It seems long ago. The rap of my stick on the pavement startles a colony of rabbits in a field on the edge of town. The thin dirt trail winds up out of this narrow valley. High cirrus clouds are visible in the transitioning sky; they'll vaporize soon enough.

I forgot my water bottle.

Distracted about leaving Sam behind, I walked out without my stick and had to run back up the stairs to retrieve it. Now this. I do some quick math on distance already covered and that which needs to be traveled to the first town. I stop. I'm torn over whether to go back or not.

My eye is drawn up to a lone bird riding a thermal above the ridge ahead. It appears motionless in the sky, the embodiment of something utterly sure, utterly self-possessed. A beacon. Forgetting all else, I walk toward the bird, never taking my eyes from it. The bird never flaps its wings. It does not move position in the air. I pass under it, looking up. Then I'm walking backward, watching it still frozen in the sky. Finally, I turn away. Glancing over my shoulder one last time, I watch as the bird dips the tip of a wing and sweeps off over the ridge and is gone from sight.

"Thank you," I say aloud.

Tales of guardians are legion on the Camino; you can choose to see them or not, believe in them or not. I tend to be somewhat ambivalent on the topic, but on this morning it feels as if my attention was summoned, my anxieties over drinking-water and doubts about leaving Sam dispelled, and that I was sent on my way, feeling connected, inspired even. My steps are light, the sun has broken the horizon behind me, and the predawn coolness is in the past.

When the trail kicks me onto a narrow, buckling tarmac, I come upon a road sign facing the other direction. On its back, the words "trouble ahead" have been crudely scratched in small, uneven block letters. A feeling of dread passes over me. An omen? A warning to be heeded? If I'm going to believe in one kind of message from the Camino, don't I have to believe in all of them?

Passing through the well-kept and sleepy town of Castrojeriz, four obnoxious bikers run me off the road just as I'm about to cross the Río Odrilla. "*Buen Camino!*" the last in line shouts, laughing.

"*Mal Camino!*" I shout back.

It's 9:30 in the morning, and the sun is now a significant factor. The trail climbs back out of this valley, at its crest the already expansive Meseta suddenly triples in breadth.

"Wow," I whisper.

What's different about the Meseta from the last time I was here is that now there is a wide dirt track running more or less straight through the entire thing. Last time, there were long stretches of narrow footpaths snaking over sun-cracked earth between shafts of scorched wheat, creating a more solitary and precarious sensation. It was on just such a rat's tail of a trail in this exact section of the Meseta a quarter century ago that I fell into uncontrollable sobs.

I dropped to my knees, hurled my walking stick aside, cursed whatever God I half believed in, and convulsed on the ground until my body ached. I had no idea what had provoked my meltdown. All I knew was that the burden I was carrying—a burden I couldn't even name—that I had been carrying for as long as I could remember, was finally too much to bear. I was overpowered, defeated, and I surrendered. I was a failure. Lost. Alone.

When my tears subsided, I found myself on the hot, hard, ground amid scraggly shafts of wheat. I crawled to retrieve my pack, which I must have thrown off in my frenzy, and then my stick. For several unthinking hours, I walked until I came to a village, found a bed, and fell into twelve dreamless hours of sleep. The next day I awoke, hoisted my pack, and walked on. As I did, I felt as if I had forgotten something. I checked, then rechecked my pack, but could find nothing missing. After a few hours, I stopped for a rest by the side of a barn. I ate a piece of cheese on a slab of stale bread and noticed that everything around me seemed brighter: the red of the nearby tractor, the burnt umber of the earth, the azure of the sky. I could hear birdsong, clear and distinct. Then it dawned on me what I didn't have, what I had left without that morning, what I couldn't find in my pack. Fear—it occurred to me by the side of that barn—was absent. Fear had become such a pervasive vine running through my life that I had not been aware of its existence until that moment of its first absence.

It changed everything. And while fear is a cunning foe, returning like seeping water relentless in its pursuit to find a way into any crevasse, my sudden awareness of its viselike grip on my life had loosened its hold. It would never rule me in the same unconscious, dictatorial fashion again.

My Camino was different after that. What had up to that point been a slog became a romp. Where I was lonely before, I met fascinating people. Previously uninteresting history became fascinating. If before I had been half asleep, I was suddenly wide awake.

It is because of this moment that I have always wanted to return to northern Spain. And while I possess deep gratitude for that life-changing experience, I'm hoping to skate through this part of the trail today with just a good sweat.

After two more hours under the sun, a speck of green appears at the vanishing point. I continue walking, and the speck becomes trees. A thin road crosses the trail. A man in a clean white shirt is leaning against a clean white taxi in the single pool of shade. He's smiling, offering a ride to the next town . . . to Santiago . . . to the airport leading home. I nod greeting and don't break stride. Get behind me, Satan.

The small and impatient man behind the bar of a functional restaurant in a dust-covered village—the name of which I don't even bother to learn—makes me a delicious bocadillo de jamón, and I settle on the outdoor porch. James, the pilgrim dandy we met a day earlier with the feather in his hat and the twenty Caminos under his belt, comes striding up the dirt road and joins me.

Although it's not easy to see where James's proclivities lie, he flirts with a young German woman, who refuses his entreaties to join us. And then Sam, shirtless and shuffling, comes into view. He is without his walking stick.

"Have you eaten anything?" I call as he stumbles into the dusty courtyard.

"No."

"You need some water?"

"I guess," he says, irritated by my questions.

"Sit," I say, and go inside to get him something.

When I return with a large bottle of water, Sam is seated, staring into the middle distance, elbows on his knees. He still has his backpack on.

"Here, take off your pack." I go to give him a hand.

"I got it." He pushes my hand away.

"You didn't eat breakfast?"

"Stop."

"I ordered you a bocadillo."

"I don't want one. I'll get something." He guzzles a liter of water.

James finishes his lunch and, either oblivious to the tension between Sam and me or simply gracious, offers a happy wave.

"See you down the road, Sam!" he calls out and then saunters on.

Since this is the first place along the way that doesn't have any of the ice cream that Sam likes, he declines to eat anything.

"Lose your stick?"

"I forgot it."

"I did too. Had to go back and get it," I say.

"I was too far once I remembered."

Our exchange is clipped, short.

"You can get another."

"I don't think I want one."

For some reason, I'm hurt by this comment. "Well, you gotta eat something before we go. It's still a long way."

The small man who runs the bar, so matter-of-fact with me, is patient and understanding as Sam finally settles on a half dozen cans of tuna fish. Sam wolfs down a can and stuffs the rest in his pack. I remind him to refill his water bottle as I go to the bathroom, and then we hit the dirt road.

It's immediately evident that Sam hasn't recovered or replenished himself enough. He begins to lag behind me. He neglected to refill his water bottle, and I offer him some of the one I just bought. He refuses. We crest a small ridge and are greeted by a strong and hot wind. It's the first time we've encountered such a blow, and it's howling in our faces. At just after 2:00 p.m, the temperature is well over a hundred degrees. We pass a small sign telling us it is 424 kilometers to Santiago. Sam drops farther behind. I go back to attend to him. I offer water again.

"I'm good," he snaps.

I snap back. "Drink the fucking water, Sam. You'll die out here."

"I'm fine."

"You're not fine. You're a mess. You didn't eat. You're not taking care of yourself. Drink the water. And"—I throw in for good measure—"you forgot your stick."

Sam stops short. "I'm not gonna do this!" he screams.

"Do what?"

"All of it! I'm not gonna do it! I'm done!"

Done with what, exactly? The walk? More probably he's talking about all of it—parent and child. Assertion vs. rebellion. Right and wrong. Father/son. The power struggle. Relationships. The whole thing. Fuck it. Sam just wants out. His face is deeply red, in equal parts from the sun and emotion. He's glaring at me. There are dirt fields to the right and left. The land is barren, played out.

There's nothing to do but make it to the next village. There is no other option. There we might hope to find that white taxi or one like it, just "tap out," and hope we can justify it enough to live with it. The other choice is to take care and trudge on through it, get to the other side. The challenge for a parent in any given situation is to know just how much lead to offer, how and when to intervene, when not to, and when to know it's just none of your business.

"OK," I say softly.

I turn and leave Sam to it.

After a few minutes, I glance over my shoulder. Sam is already several hundred yards behind. He's taken off his shirt again and is weaving slowly along the dusty track. He stumbles and rights himself just before he falls. I bend to retie my already well-knotted shoe. The sun burns on my back like a hot iron. I stand and slowly take out my water to have a small sip. When Sam arrives, I ask him, "Will you put this back in my pack? I can't reach it."

He takes the bottle. "Can I have a sip?"

"Of course."

He swigs deeply. Then goes to replace it in the side pocket of my pack.

"Take some more."

He does. We stand in the sun and meet eyes. Sam holds my look. We walk on together.

Two black birds chase each other across the sky. Then an aqueduct overflowing with water appears from nowhere. A small patch of robust corn, its green leaves draping languorously amid an otherwise blistered expanse of brown earth. A square patch of bounty amid deprivation.

Sam begins to talk softly about The Ex. When I asked about her recently, Sam informed me, "I'll talk about it when I need to." I haven't brought it up since. But now, in ripping wind, under skin-peeling heat, dehydrated, starving, exhausted, it seems to be the moment.

By the time wind and sun have blown and burned away Sam's angst, we are walking over parched land again. On our left is an expanse of cut wheat, the earth cracked and caked hard. I spot a small break in the withered growth dividing the farmland and road. On impulse, I slip off the wide dirt track we've been slaves to and head out into the field.

"Where are you going?" Sam asks.

Just a few yards from the road, the freedom of forging our own path is a revelation. The feeling of liberation creates physical buoyancy. We begin to laugh, then run, our packs bouncing and jostling, creating more laughter. Then Sam is singing.

On the outskirts of Boadilla del Camino there is a large and flowing fountain. We sloppily fill our bottles like kings at a banquet and chug the cool water down. Then we fill them again. Sam holds up his refilled bottle for a toast. We tap plastic.

He grins. "The Meseta is a piece of cake."

"That's not a good idea"

268 miles to Santiago

I get the impression that it's only because Eduardo has good impulse control that he refrains from giving Sam a good smack upside the head. Eduardo is thin, with a week's growth of beard, wears a wool cap pushed back on his head, and is in possession of a strong work ethic and street English. Sam has just asked for his second cup of morning coffee in a "to go" cup.

"You're too fancy for us," Eduardo tells him by way of dismissal. "Too fancy." Just a few minutes earlier, Sam had been slumped in a chair in the lobby of our hotel, scrolling his phone as I served him his first cup of coffee. He had been slumped in the same chair on our arrival while I checked us in. And when I ordered him a Coke, and when I asked about where we might find Sam's daily hit of ice cream. Eduardo had watched it all without comment. He had also acted as our waiter at dinner. Eduardo does everything at his simple hotel, as well as at the albergue next door, the only two places to stay in Boadilla del Camino.

"We're gonna keep you here for a few weeks," he says to Sam. "No phone, just work."

Sam offers a wan smile and gulps his coffee down.

That I wait on Sam too much is certain. Partly it's out of pleasure, and in a large part it's just easier in order to get things done more quickly and efficiently. Either way, it's bad parenting and bone-deep behavior.

After Sam's traumatic birth, he spent the first five days of his life in the neonatal intensive care unit. Sucking is one of the first signs of brain function and normalcy in a newborn—and for days, Sam didn't. Lying in an incubator, he was connected by wires to beeping monitors. Sam was fed intravenously, but he needed to begin to eat on his own. For hours I sat with my son in my lap, trying to feed him with an eye dropper. On the third day, I thought I saw Sam swallow a drop I put in his mouth. I squeezed another, then another. Then the eye dropper was empty. Sam was eating. I was crying. And our dynamic was established.

Upstairs, a few minutes prior to the coffee incident, Sam lay under the covers. I told him I was leaving. It was just after 7:00 a.m., our previously agreed-on departure time. The heat was forecast to be even more intense today. An early start was imperative.

"So, you sleep," I said. "I'll see you down the road."

"You said that's not a good idea."

"I don't think it is. But I'm not looking for a fight, and it's time to go. It's just a few more days in the Meseta."

I left.

"I'll be there in five minutes," Sam called as the door closed behind me.

Two dirty white horses try to graze in a lifeless soccer field with a rusted goalpost, its net long gone. A giant fireball sun is cresting the horizon behind us. We pick up a smooth, tree-lined path beside an eighteenth-century canal tracking due west. The air is still cool, and the walking is easy.

"Good to be out early," I say.

"You know, Dad," Sam says, "it actually is."

We talk flat earth, social arrangements, the glory of Elvis.

"What's so amazing about him?"

"You can't understand it now. He was so far out in front of what society was doing. And it was all just impulse. But no one could sustain in that kind of leading-edge exposure."

Ahead, sitting on a pressure valve beside the canal, the unmistakable figure of James—he of the long black robe and feathered hat and twenty Caminos—is seated in imitation of Rodin's famous *Thinker* pose, staring into the water.

"James!" Sam calls out.

Our friend is in a pensive mood.

"You sleep outside the church last night?" I ask. "It was chilly."

"I'm so ashamed," James says.

"Why?" Sam asks.

"I slept in the hotel." He looks down.

"Ahhh." Sam nods in understanding.

"But they were nice beds," I say.

"They were!" James cries. "And the shower, ahhhhhh."

"Your secret is safe with us," I tell him.

"Yeah," Sam adds. "You gotta keep up your Camino cred."

"I appreciate that, men." James plays along. We leave him to ponder the canal.

In Frómista, a classic Camino market town, there's a small eleventh-century Romanesque church—Iglesia de San Martín. I have a distinct recollection of the simple arched building sitting far off by itself, alone in the dust, and my seeking out the man with the key to allow me a look inside. In an effort to honor the mysterious randomness of what memory deems important, I've looked forward to repeating the action.

I find the church itself much as I remember it, but it is surrounded by pavement and shops and a farmer's market, in the center of commerce. The resonant charm of a solitary house of worship built by devout believers in the middle of a sandy bit of nowhere is absent; it's just a pretty, old building encircled by asphalt. Is my recollection a victim of progress or is it just faulty memory?

Sam and I eat breakfast at a café in the church's shadow. We're joined by James, and when I suggest that things have changed, he shrugs. "This is how it's always been since I've been walking," James says. "Things could certainly have changed from when you walked the Camino that long ago."

I know James isn't implying anything about my age, but simply being polite and allowing for time to alter things. "I envy you those quiet days on the Camino."

Sam is having none of it. "You're just old, Dad." Then perhaps feeling himself a little harsh, Sam continues. "But you're looking the silver fox, Dad. To be sure."

"You're making it worse, Sam."

I make no effort at a look inside the locked church. We buy some peaches at a market stall and walk on.

Not far out of the village, the Camino splits. One trail leads off under trees and follows an indirect course beside the Río Ucieza. It's a slightly longer adjunct to the primary trail that tracks the main road all the way for eleven charmless, shadeless miles. For the only time across Spain, I suggest we split up. I'm grateful for the Camino's timing in so quickly offering Sam an opportunity to be well prepared and put his solo struggles from yesterday behind him. With food in his stomach, water, and snacks in his pack, and knowing Sam's preference for a straight shot and mine for a more pleasant one, it's an easy suggestion. Without breaking stride, we bump fists, and I veer off over a footbridge.

I pass rows of planted pines, cross another footbridge, and pick up the river. At one point I slip off the trail and slide down between trees and sit beside the water, protected from view. Without movement, I can feel myself vibrating internally. My usual mixed emotions of missing my son while simultaneously being grateful for the solitude are slightly but paternally modified as Sam rewrites his way through the Meseta—stepping out on his own, at least for a few hours.

Long after the soft morning has become the brutal afternoon, I come upon my son on the outskirts of Carrión. He's sitting on the curb in the

ANDREW MCCARTHY

sun, ten feet from a large patch of shade, red faced, shirt off, waiting. I
can see immediately that he's had a solid afternoon.

"Good walk?" I ask.

"Yeah. Hot."

In its heyday, Carrión de los Condes was home to ten thousand residents. It's dwindled to less than a quarter that number today. Like many
towns along the Camino, it has a bloody past. This is where El Cid took
revenge with his trusty sword, Tizona, and slaughtered a few counts foolish enough to have mistreated his daughters. And it was in Carrión that
the price of one hundred local Christian virgins was paid each year, until
the faithful prayed hard enough and a herd of bulls ran off the cursed
Moors who had oppressed them.

I wouldn't mind a similar stampede when we come upon Irish playing
a harmonica with shrill enthusiasm and drinking beer with a drunken
Portuguese man just off the Plaza de Santa María. Sam extracts himself
to go work out down at the river, and I have any number of things to
do—I just can't remember any off the top of my head, since my brain is
so baked by the heat. It doesn't matter; Irish and his companion are so
drunk they don't notice us leave.

I'd agreed that we would meet James for dinner in the Plaza del Gen-
eralísimo Franco (Carrión is one of the few towns to still boast the name
of the Fascist dictator), but by then my mood is sour. I'm tired. I miss my
wife and my other kids. I'm in no spirit for chat. Sam is sullen over The
Ex. He just wants to go get pizza.

"Look, we'll eat quick and get it over with," I tell him.

There's only one restaurant with a table available, and that's because
the patio is in the evening sun.

"Fuck," I mutter.

Then I hear my name. The Boys, Ryan and Chris, come marching up,
beaming. They, along with Irish, were the first people we met along The
Way. We haven't seen them since outside Logroño, where we stopped for a

rest day. It's as if during our time apart, we have walked into a friendship. The feeling is of reconnecting with a more innocent version of ourselves. Seeing each other now speaks to our own progress along the road: we're reminded of how far we've all come, are grateful for the safe passage so far, and are brought up-to-date. I invite them to join us. They're accompanied by the sad-eyed Hungarian woman, Erika. James arrives in a flurry, and we all cram around a small table on the patio. The sun no longer seems so invasive.

The talk is easy and loud. As conversations overlap, Erika, who is about thirty, tells me that her husband died of cancer nearly a year ago. She is walking to be in Santiago on the anniversary of his death. She carries her story loosely, offering it freely. Then she shifts her attention back to Ryan, who treats her with tenderness. Chris is playful. James is interested in Sam, peppering him with questions on his life and how he finds walking the Camino. He pulls out a pouch of tobacco.

"Can I have one of those?" Sam asks.

James hands Sam the pouch and a rolling paper. Sam fumbles with the tobacco and tears the paper.

"Takes a bit of practice," James assures him.

Then James orders a bottle of wine and asks my permission for Sam to have a glass.

"Ask Sam," I say.

"I'll have a taste," Sam says and introduces the topic of his recent breakup. I'm surprised by this but reminded again that Sam is a very different person than I am—that so many of my projections onto him are merely that, my own projections. In the company of others, it's sometimes easier to see those we love more clearly—as if through their eyes.

"Yeah, it's been intense," he says. "We've been talking about it. Right, Dad?" I nod and keep silent, careful that my voice does not intrude. Sam's simple openness takes the table to a deeper level of casual intimacy. His unapologetic nature claims his space as an equal. Chris and Ryan offer their own stories of heartache and resilience.

The food is poor, and it doesn't matter. Over the course of the meal, and a few glasses of wine, Sam grows more expansive. It's a rare parental privilege to watch your child come of age before your eyes. James presses Sam on what it's like to walk with his father.

Something in James's question cuts through the other conversations around the table, and it grows quiet, everyone now looking to Sam. He ponders his reply, his head nodding slowly. I wait along with the others. I have no idea what Sam might say, and because of my own state of relaxation can make the internal choice to simply wait and see, without tensing under defensive anticipation.

"It's good," Sam says at last. His conclusion encapsulates the consideration of weeks on the hoof up to this moment. It is decisive. It's a complete answer.

The seriousness with which Sam took the question invites others to contemplate their own paternal relationships.

"I never would have done this with my father," Chris says. Ryan agrees. So does James.

"I wouldn't have either," I say.

"Well," Sam begins again slowly. "It's been helpful. I'm glad we're doing it." He stops and nods again. "Yeah."

I make no outward reaction, but it would be difficult for me to feel prouder. Then Sam begins talking about being the child of divorce.

"I say this with all the love in the world, but I don't want my kid to go back and forth between two houses. It's been great for me, and it's taught me to be resilient and adaptable, but...yeah."

My puffed ego slips in the quicksand of my fallibility. I reach over and squeeze Sam's shoulder.

"Love you, Dad."

The light around the square has faded. The empty plates are taken away. James offers Sam a cigar—a big fat one.

"I've smoked one cigar," Sam says, "with my stepdad."

Sam's stepfather is a good man, a solid and decent one. "An old-school boomer," is how Sam once described Joe with affection. He's offered Sam a perspective I couldn't. Just as Dolores offers Sam something his mom doesn't. "It takes a village to raise Sam," Dolores once remarked after the four adults consulted on a Sam-related mini-crisis—to which everyone echoed agreement.

James fires up the cigars.

As the long meal ends, we are the last in the restaurant, and the late-summer sky is long dark. Most pilgrims are already tucked in for the night. When we part, James grabs my arm. He looks me in the eye and nods gravely. "Nice job, Dad."

I have to look away.

Sam and I stroll back to our hotel. He's still expansive and a little more than tipsy. At the river, several young teens are jumping off the bridge into the water twenty feet below. We shout encouragement. They ask where we're from.

"Nueva York!" Sam calls back.

"Whoa!" they shout, and splash down into the river.

"This ain't no dream"

253 miles to Santiago

There are some things that a parent will put up with in their offspring that no one else ever would. We do it out of love, because we find our kids charming, or because we want to support them in the full expression of who they are, or maybe because we just want them to like us. But sometimes it is all we can do not to scream "Please shut the fuck up!"

Sam is singing a single line from a Bruce Springsteen song, over and over. This is my fault—it is payback for all the years I inflicted the Bard of New Jersey on members of my household. I would take it all back now if I could. We are walking over a disused asphalt strip that points straight to the horizon. An unfinished trench for an abandoned canal tracks the road. The sun is rising behind us, over a gas station.

Finally, I correct Sam, who has been singing the line wrong.

"Really?" he asks.

"Yeah, it's 'Strung out on the *wire*...'"

"Huh."

"Kind of the way I feel right now."

We are walking over what is perhaps the most uninspired terrain of the entire Camino de Santiago. Plowed fields. Fields abandoned. Dried swampland. Flat. Even my guidebooks, which are always upbeat and finding more interesting aspects of the walk than I could ever take in, are defeated by this landscape. One euphemistically calls it "somewhat featureless," while the other just flat-out gives up and deems it "a slog." My own notes describe this morning's walk as "dire."

Anticipating more heat today, we left before the café was open. That we are walking without caffeine does not help the situation. In what passes for excitement, the tarmac quits and the trail becomes dirt. This is apparently the old Roman road. Whatever. For ten and a half miles there is no town, no diversion. No shade. The only hope for relief comes in the form of a coffee truck that is reportedly camped six miles down the trail.

By 8:30, the sun is already a foe. In time, we see a small strand of trees on the horizon. Moving closer, we see that a cute, out-of-date, camper has been unhitched and propped up on cinder block. There are a few white plastic tables and chairs set up in the unkempt, overdried grass. Maybe not an oasis, but relief.

Sam heads directly for a chair and drops his load. "I'll have two black coffees."

"Oh, good."

Earlier, Sam confessed to having "A tiny bit of a headache."

"You play, you pay." I shrugged.

"It was a good night, though."

"It was a great night, Sammy," I corrected him.

It was the night Sam stepped from my shadow and took possession of his own Camino.

I stand in line behind a single pilgrim. There are a half dozen other walkers, none of whom I recognize, at the tables. The woman ahead of me gets her four coffees and, balancing them, slowly moves off to her friends.

"*Dos café negro y uno café con leche, por favor,*" I say.

"*No más,*" the young man in the camper says through the open window.

"What?"

There is no more coffee. I explain that I just saw the woman in front of me carry four coffees. I even point at her. He shrugs. They were the last.

My jaw hangs open for a not insignificant amount of time. How about some juice, the friendly man in the camper suggests.

Sam and I sit slumped in the plastic chairs with our warm juice in the sun. Defeated. I tell him we need to get going.

"No," he says.

"We have to go," I repeat.

Sam shakes his head. Like a dog refusing to go out in the rain, he will not be swayed. A child I would have to cajole, coax, convince. Even earlier in the Camino, I would have tried to persuade him. But Sam is no longer a child, and it is not early in the Camino. I pick up my pack and start off.

The sun is ferocious. Soon enough I can hear Sam pounding up the trail behind me, singing his hangover away at the top of his lungs, gaining on me. At the uninspired village of Calzadilla de la Cueza, an amiable man feeds and waters us. On we go, finally hitting our stride for the day. Sam talks the zombie apocalypse.

"Why are people obsessed with zombies? When did the entire culture become so juvenile?" I ask.

Sam ignores my stodgy indignation. "It'll feel like this, bro," indicating the stark, desolate, peopleless landscape.

Then, as we come out of a small bend in the trail beyond a knoll, the vista is altered.

"Oh, look," I say in earnest surprise. "It's a different color brown."

While traveling over such featureless land void of distraction it's easy to feel the unspoken yet palpable solidarity in our walking this afternoon— a result of the active goodwill created by last night's dinner. Any intimacy eventually benefits from the company of society in order that its reflection be cast back upon itself for perspective.

A band of religious warriors and Crusaders, the Knights Templar had a mission to protect pilgrims along the way to Santiago during the twelfth to the fourteenth century. They were bloodthirsty, feared, revered, and brought down in disgrace. History has treated them with a mixture of reverence and revulsion. The dying village of Terradillos de los Templarios, our home for the night, is named in their honor.

It's difficult to imagine what the reviled and venerated knights would have made of the four girls washing their hair in the fountain outside the town's crumbling brick church, or of our lodging, by the side of the N-120. Sitting behind a mesh fence, it is without immediate charm. But as with all albergues along the Way, the quality of the stay depends less on the degree of services than the pilgrims one encounters and the personality of the person in charge. In this case, a thin, black-haired woman bearing a striking resemblance to the singer Patti Smith is easy and accommodating, and seemingly everywhere at once. Isabel is offhanded and upbeat, and like anyone who runs a pilgrim hostel, a workhorse. She is also patient with Sam's exacting requests regarding his laundry.

Spread out on the veranda and front lawn, a dozen pilgrims lounge in clusters and drink beer, tend to blistered feet, or nap. Even after a grind such as today, there is satisfaction in arrival and completion of the day's walk. The Boys, Ryan and Chris, are here, as is their friend from Hungry, Erika. So is Theresa, the physiotherapist from Belgium, whom I met walking out of Burgos. So are a few others I recognize.

While Sam fills his backpack with rocks and does lateral raises in the sun, the rest of us gather at a table in the shade, and the topic shifts to a Camino favorite—the life-changing things learned while walking. "I'm going to take my new meditation practice into my daily life," says one. "I've learned to plan less," says another. And the tightly wound physiotherapist from Belgium assures the group that she has "learned to let go of control." (Not long ago in Burgos, it was her expectations that she jettisoned. Theresa certainly seems to be making progress in the self-improvement category.) Whenever I hear people talk about the profound insights they've gained while walking the Camino while they are still walking the Camino, I'm always slightly embarrassed. These claims strike me as a kind of desperate grasping for meaning and contain a childish one-upmanship. I go to take my laundry down off the line out back and wonder why I'm such a jaded and cynical bastard.

At dinner, when Isabel presents me with a plate of white asparagus, I ask if she's familiar with Patti Smith.

She shakes her head. "Should I be?"

I like her even more, and I decide in this instant that I too need to run an albergue—if only there were anything about the service industry that appealed to me.

"Did you grab my laundry off the line?" Sam asks me as he dips into his soup.

I conclude that waiting on my son hand and foot is enough service for me.

"It sure takes a while"

"It's like all my life I've been waiting for this or that to happen, and then I'll be happy. Like it's just out there." Sam reaches his hand out in front of him. "I mean, I'm really enjoying the Camino, but part of me can't wait to be done so that whatever is gonna happen can happen. I think in my relationship it was the first time I wasn't doing that."

The sun is not yet over the horizon line. We're just past a small cluster of solar panels, picking up a straight track flanked on one side by poplar trees and a narrow strip of asphalt on the other. Isabel made us a cup of smooth, strong coffee and, as of yesterday, we are halfway to Santiago de Compostela, so why not get right into it.

"Yeah, that's one of the most amazing things about love. Its power to joyfully grab you by the throat and ground you firmly in the present. Which then usually fills you with gratitude, and it feels like you can see something no one else does. Like you know the secret."

"Exactly."

I consider mentioning that I had these same feelings regarding Sam's mother when I met her at eighteen in college. It was the first time I was in love, and the world opened up for me in a similar fashion to what Sam has just been describing. Perhaps I should tell him, perhaps that's the kind of openness this adult-to-adult relationship begs for at this point. But fearing this will be upsetting for my son to hear, I refrain.

I pick up on his other point. "The thinking 'next, next,' I understand that one. But the thing about that is, all that thinking about what's next is a trick to keep us from the present. And the feeling of vulnerability and precariousness that exists in the now." Pointing to the field beside us, where giant bales of hay are stacked high into towers, some leaning at impossible angles, I continue. "You kind of feel like you're sitting on top of that stack of tilting hay. Like you're gonna go over at any second."

"And if you're gonna be in the present, you also have to accept where you are," Sam says.

"True."

"But," Sam argues, "on the other hand, if you have an assumption about your future reality, it can happen."

Before I can ask what he means, Sam goes on.

"Look at Matthew McConaughey. He assumed he was gonna be famous. He saw it for himself."

"Well, yeah. I mean, how else could you explain it?"

"Oh, Dad. Envy?"

"I couldn't resist."

We enter the tiny settlement of Moratinos. In this part of the Meseta, stone is rare, and we begin to see houses made of mud—earthen walls with occasional small pieces of straw protruding. Then, just as quickly, the village is behind us. Mountains are visible far to the north.

"I'm really looking forward to having my own apartment," Sam says. "I don't mean this in any bad way, but I've never had a place. Always going back and forth between you and Mom. There's no 'poor me,' but to have a place to settle…"

Of course, I've known that shuttling between two households—week on, week off—for nearly his entire life has had an effect on Sam. It always took a few days for that edge he'd arrive with to vanish, and then all too soon he'd be gone again. Daily phone calls never quite bridged that void. But I've been surprised how much the topic has come up on the Camino, what a factor it still is.

"I hear you," I say. "I obviously can't compare or ever really know what that felt like, Sammy, but I do remember moving into my first place on my own. The relief."

Standing in my first solo apartment, I closed the door and looked around. It contained a mattress I had found on the street and dragged up two flights and the stained, threadbare corner piece of a sectional sofa my parents were throwing out. I sat down on the floor in the middle of the room and let out a sigh I had been holding my entire life.

Sam is silent for a time. "It sure takes a while, doesn't it?"

"What does?"

Sam says nothing.

"All of it?" I prod my son.

The walk? Growing up? Getting over relationships? Getting to know someone—like your son?

Sam finally speaks. His tone is wistful. "Yeah, I guess."

Just outside the village of San Nicolas del Reál Camino, we come upon a primitively hand-painted sign attached to a telephone pole reading, "I know I don't know anything, but I know the second bar is best." The quote is attributed to Socrates. Taken so off guard by this attribution, I burst into uproarious laughter.

Just around the bend and on the edge of town, the first café we come to is attractive and inviting, but the advertising has worked, and we walk on to the second bar. We're glad we do.

Laganares, on the tiny Plaza Mayor adjacent to the Iglesia de San Nicolás Obispo, has been refurbished using the local mud-and-straw method. The window boxes overflow with purple and white petunias. Half a dozen tables and chairs with red-checked tablecloths sit out front, in the shade of a few mature poplar trees. Sam and I are the only patrons at the moment. Our hosts are a husband-and-wife team, the Huidobros. She makes us the best omelets we have eaten in Spain, and he draws the smoothest coffees. There's a slight breeze in the shade. The church bell rings out. There are moments when life seems to make the kind of sense we often wish it made—when the universe seems to sit in our lap, when things are revealed in a simplicity of being and unity. They are moments that add up to more than the sum of their parts—moments of serendipity when things come together in a meeting of circumstance, timing, and mood. It's impossible to predict or plan or fully explain such times. They defy efforts at repeating, even if all outward elements are the same. That they seem more common in travel than at home is one of the primary reasons people like me bother to go anywhere in the first place.

We sit for far too long. I get up so contented that even walking on the side of the N-120 highway into the province of León and all the way to Sahagún can't dampen my mood.

Once a powerhouse of Christianity and an anchor for this part of the Camino, Sahagún is filled with churches old and older, ruins, monasteries, and the remains of martyred saints. It's a hustle-bustle crossroads today, and Sam is ready to keep walking right on through. But I have some idea that I liked this place last time—although nothing seems familiar—and insist we stop for lunch. At a café on the rough and tumble Plaza Mayor, our waiter tells us that we want some jamón de León, a local delicacy.

"*Muy fuerte*," he assures us. And it is—strong and sweet and quickly gone. But town and the midday heat have cast a pall over our carefree moods. We cross the Río Cea over the Puente Canto. A sprinkler is watering a gaudy field of corn, diabolical in its lushness among such desolate environs. We divert to let the water douse us. It's then that I feel a burning sensation in one of my toes.

"You go on, Sammy. I gotta tend to this."

"You sure?"

I know Sam likes to power ahead after lunch, and he stands shifting his weight from one foot to the next.

"Yeah. Go on. I'll catch up."

I drop to the ground, kick off my shoe, and peel back my sock. "Oh, fuck." I have three blisters. When I finally look up, Sam is lost from view. For the next seven miles, the narrow dirt trail is bound on one side by small trees that provide scant shade, and on the other by a forsaken road. Heat rises off the tarmac.

I'm sure it's simply because I've heard Sam expound too much on his theories regarding altered planes of existence and perceptions of reality, but when the only car I encounter the entire walk, an aqua-and-yellow Peugeot dating from the 1960s, passes me, I'm disoriented enough to—for a moment—question where the hell I am and exactly what the fuck is happening. Or maybe it's just the sun.

Sam is waiting for me, as he always is when he walks ahead, on the edge of town. There are times when I come upon him that he appears like an anxious puppy, eager for his bowl to be filled; at other times, he's more like an impatient proctor awaiting a delinquent charge. But at present, with his shirt off, sunburned back, thumb hitched through the strap on his pack flung lightly over one shoulder, Sam strikes me as nothing so much as a contented Camino warrior.

"I could eat," he says as I arrive.

We land in Bercianos del Real Camino amid La Fiesta de la Asunción, and the celebration appears to be centered around the family bar/pensión where we're staying. Most of the town's two hundred inhabitants are here. We're incorporated into the proceedings with little fanfare. Sam orders a plate of pasta Bolognese, I stick to jamón and melon. Surrounded by young and old dressed in casual and festive attire, we swill Coke and try to stop sweating. Teenage girls cluster, whispering, giggling. Boys in football jerseys make a show of casually drinking beer and strut past. One of the girls reaches out and slaps the lead boy's behind. He knows his friends have seen. He ignores her, a smirk on his face. Women are assembled around the tables. Men crowd the dark bar. Outside, a teenage boy has been assigned to monitor a toddler, dutifully walking him up and down, even tousling his hair.

"How's the Bolognese?" I ask.

"Um...can I have some of your jamón?"

I push the plate over.

"Did you think you were suddenly in Rome?"

An hour later, the place is deserted. Everyone has gone home to wait out the one-hundred-and-four-degree heat.

Because it lacks an old center and a galvanizing town square, there's an out-of-time-and-space quality about Bercianos. Walking through the deserted town in the heat, there's little obvious charm other than the intermittent mud-and-straw house built among more contemporary stucco-and-brick functionality. An old lady sits in the doorway of her home, out of the sun, keeping an eye on the empty street. Watching me pass, she wears a disapproving look. When I call out a greeting, the brittle mask of her face breaks, and her voice is warm and friendly. At El Sueve bar, on the edge of town, across from long-abandoned earthen dwellings, three tables are filled with old men hunched over dominos, clicking tiles the only sound. The town's most prominent feature is a massive and modern steel scaffolding clocktower that was erected when the church collapsed in 1998. It sits off in the sun like a folly. Sam circles it, gesticulating wildly, appearing to talk with himself—Don Quixote tilting at windmills.

"Everything all right back home?" I ask Sam at dinner.

"Yeah, The Ex's birthday is coming up. She wants me to do a birthday post. Says it will look weird if I don't."

"But you guys have broken up."

"Well, she's told people we're just taking a break for the summer."

"Ooooooooh," I say slowly. "Is that your understanding?"

"No. Obviously." His mood is remarkably sanguine. "My friends will kill me if I cave and do it." Our food arrives. "I'm really thinking I might go to Finisterre."

"It's three days' walk beyond Santiago."

"I'd do it in two."

"All right."

"But I might not."

I'd love for him to go to Finisterre. I'd hate for him to make that post.

"Any opinions, Dad?"

"I've got blisters to worry about."

"It seems dumb"

222 miles to Santiago

I spend a pointless half hour walking around in the dark, searching for coffee. Add to this that it is not just cool this morning, but cold. I turn left, then right, shivering, cursing. I can't locate a bar. Sam is still asleep, warm under the covers. "What the fuck am I doing?" I say aloud. Giving up, I head back to our pensión. I climb the dark stairs. I pop the lock.

"You got coffee, bro?" Sam mumbles from beneath the covers.

If I had any I'd pour it on him.

After a few weeks of trouble-free feet, this morning my blisters from yesterday are worse. I now count six, in various stages of development. The heat of the Meseta has caused my feet to sweat, and now trouble feeds trouble. I spend the half hour it takes to rouse Sam tending to them—while trying to quell my as yet unspoken fear that I might have to stop for a few days to let them subside.

The trail today is the same as yesterday. Seventeen miles on a flat and narrow track flanked by immature sycamore trees and a narrow strip of asphalt. The heatwave has broken, just as we are leaving what is traditionally the hottest part of the Meseta. As it always does, the walking is quick to burn away anxiety and stress, and my mood lifts. We walk in lockstep.

Ahead on the trail, two figures are on the ground. Getting closer, we see The Boys, Ryan and Chris, just getting up from a break. Sam falls in between them; I walk close behind on the pinched trail. A decade younger than the two friends, Sam is happy for the new company. I'm caught off guard at how easily he dives into the center of their conversation without hesitation or restraint and am reminded once again of the inaccuracy of my own projections. I'm also aware of just how important it is for Sam that he be treated as an adult, and I'm attuned to whether The Boys are accepting him as an equal. To that end, I'm also hypervigilant for any perceived overreaches or missteps by my son that might put them off and on several occasions hold back from intervening or massaging the conversation. It's odd, especially since I admire Sam's confidence and think so highly of him and do all I can to support his passions and nurture his free expression, that I would be so oversensitive to his enthusiasms when expressed in the wider world. My own sense of shame has held me back both personally and professionally on countless occasions. Seeing such liberation in my son ought to bring me joy, and it does, but I first need to see beyond my own limitations.

When Chris begins to discuss the Wim Hof breathing techniques that he's been teaching Ryan and invites Sam to join their next session, it becomes clear that I ought to just mind my own business.

Having had no breakfast on the way out of town, after a few hours of walking, we're desperate. In the listless town of El Burgo Ranero, we at last find a café willing to serve us. Sam plops down outside.

"Will you please get up and order for yourself, at least?" I tell him. "I'm not here to wait on you all the time."

Sam takes no offense at this and gets up.

"You could even order for me, once in a while," I say.

"I can't speak Spanish," Sam says.

"You can say 'omelet.'"

"True."

Sam waits for our food. I sit outside. A few minutes later, Ryan and Chris, who came into the bar and ordered after us, come outside carrying two omelets. Curious, and starving, I go in. Sam is still waiting.

"Was that our food the boys just walked out with?"

"I don't know."

The owner of the bar shuffles out of the kitchen, and I ask about our eggs. He says he already made the two omelets. I point out the confusion, that there were apparently two orders of two omelets. He is angry and refuses to make two more. Seeing the panic in my eyes, he relents. Eventually, we get some food. I feel like an asshole for intervening in a situation I demanded Sam handle but tell myself this is why I do everything myself.

Whether it's my berating him in the morning to get going or accusations back home of thoughtless behavior toward one of his siblings, Sam has the ability to take in what needs to be heard—even when it appears he hasn't—and disregard the limitations, biases, or projections of the messenger. We set out again in good spirits. Past a cemetery, a picnic area, a small airstrip, our talk returns to relationships, and then marriage. I describe how much trouble comes from transferring our own crap onto our partner—just as I've been doing to Sam for much of the morning.

"It just sounds like a whole lot of not thinking clearly," Sam says.

I have little to add to that wisdom.

When we pass through an arroyo, Sam says, "I mean, I'll probably get married, but as a logical thinking, inexperienced person, it seems dumb."

In the gutter on the main street in the town of Reliegos, a half dozen plastic tables and accompanying chairs have been placed randomly in front of a typical bar. Any charm that exists is in its functionality. Reliegos's claim to fame has nothing to do with the Camino. In 1947, a forty-pound meteor landed on Calle Real (and you can visit it in the Museo Nacional de Ciencias Naturales in Madrid). We've caught up to The Boys again. Erika, the Hungarian woman, is here as well. She has blisters and is suffering badly. They're joined by a middle-aged man with a salt-and-pepper beard and sleeves of tattoos. His name is Roger. He's from Seattle and is quick to tell us that he took a taxi for the past few days. Why he did so is unclear—his admitting he did so, even more surprising. What he does make clear is that he is doing the Camino for the camaraderie. Chris, meanwhile, is holding forth on the health benefits of eating raw garlic. He produces a giant clove from his rucksack and offers it up.

"Gentlemen?"

Ryan says he's in. So is Roger. I shake my head.

"Sam?"

Sam grabs it, and they all begin chewing. I head inside to get Sam another Coke and a hunk of bread. He'll need them. The oppressive midday heat that has been the defining characteristic of the walk up to now is gone. We all sit for an extended time, feet up. Erika offers me an anti-inflammatory ointment that I put on my feet, and in an instant my life is better.

For the final four miles of the day, into Mansilla de las Mulas, Sam plugs in his headphones and charges ahead. I'm content to walk alone at a quiet and easy pace. After such combative heat, the balmy air—what my daughter, Willow, likes to call "no temperature"—is revelatory. The sun is a welcome friend instead of the tormentor it's been. Ambling along the same featureless trail we've been following for two days, I begin to experience a strange sensation, as if there is someone following me, perhaps very close behind. I resist looking over my shoulder. I pass corn-fields, and the feeling intensifies. It becomes an almost physical sensation of weight pressing down on my shoulders from behind. I'm now afraid to look. I may be hit from behind at any second. If I turn and someone is in fact there, they will scoff at me for glancing back. I press ahead. It's only getting worse. Finally, as if shoving a large weight aside, I whirl around.

There is, of course, nothing there. Only the trail and sky and fields— and the mess my mind has made.

The Meseta has been a more subtle foe this trip than the last, but I'll be glad to have it behind me tonight.

The town of Mansilla on the Río Esla still retains its large medieval walls of fortification, built in the twelfth century. It's long been an important town on The Way and the convergence point for two trails heading to Santiago. Sam and I eat well at a restaurant under a canopy of grape vines. Tomorrow is The Ex's birthday, and the expected social media post continues to be the hot topic.

"If it's just on my story, that's a whole different thing than if it's a feed post." Sam is trying to be patient with me. "Can't you get that?"

"I get it, I get it," I say, not entirely sure I get it. "But why do you have to do any post at all? Especially if you don't want to."

"Look, it'll just make my life easier."

"Yeah, but to what end? Is it being emotionally honest?"

"Come on, don't do that."

"Sammy, what else are we doing out here then? All this walking and talking?"

(Heavy sigh.) "I know. You're right..." Sam pushes back his chair.

"Where are you going?"

"I need ice cream."

"When did you know"

205 miles to Santiago

"If I had a day of no consequences," Sam says, "I'd just walk around and kill roosters."

We're crossing the elevated bridge over the Río Esla on the way out of Mansilla de las Mulas. The trail has turned north toward León. The morning sun now to our right, our long shadows climb the acacia trees to our left. A crowing and unseen rooster, Sam's nemesis across Spain, has just caught his attention.

I broke my vow and had a napolitana de chocolate with my coffee this morning. I justified this by concluding that since I am recovering from painful and worrisome blisters, I deserve some comfort. I then concluded that you can justify anything. I further decided to stop thinking for the day and enjoy the walk into León. The last larger city along The Way before Santiago, it's traditionally a place where the Camino takes a deep breath after the Meseta, then gathers itself up and pushes the pilgrim back out on the road to verdant Galicia. I have fond memories of the place.

The trail into León today grows increasingly more urban and unappealing as sprawling outskirts encroach upon the rolling fields. The Camino follows busy roads and highways. The dirt path we're on is shadowing the humming N-601.

In a wooded and secluded dip just beside the highway, we come upon a makeshift bar—tarpaulin and salvaged planks of wood tied together with rope make for walls of a sort, and a few plastic tables and chairs and a port-a-potty pass for hospitality. Such quirky places of homemade charm are not uncommon on the road to Santiago. Invariably run by Camino eccentrics, they are often worth a stop. I take no notice of the two pilgrims hurrying away with their heads down as we drop our packs. The proprietress is dressed in a flowing peasant's frock. Her long hair is equally unrestrained. "Welcome, welcome!" she calls out, spreading her arms wide. I order coffees and toast. "I have nothing to make toast with, but the bread is fresh" she tells me, then turns to set to work on the coffee, chatting while she does. "How is your Camino? What are you discovering within yourself?" Sam shoots me a look. Things begin to turn south. Our hostess is exceedingly slow and begins to pontificate on graciousness and generosity. "It binds you to the guiding force within the universe." When I ask for a second pat of butter for my stale bread, she snaps, "I can't just give away butter like it's nothing." Sam moves toward the port-a-potty. The woman stalks after him. "Do not put anything down that toilet!" Sam aborts his trip and returns to his chair. Our hostess is now ranting on the rudeness of pilgrims these days, how they have "lost purity"! On and on she goes. I catch Sam's eye and slowly move to hoist my pack. "Can we just leave?" he whispers. "Run," I whisper back. I drop too much money on the table, and we hurry away with the woman still screaming at our backs.

We walk by the side of the buzzing highway, and our talk turns to the need to prove oneself.

"I want to do something in life," Sam says.

"What do you mean?"

"Nothing. I just don't want to drift, but, like, I don't know."

One of the things my son has exhibited is a tendency to drift.

"Well, you don't have to know just yet," I say. We're silent as cars whiz past. Then, "I guess that's what I always said about why going to college can be a good thing. It gives you time, lets you transition. And if you're not going to college for a specific thing, I always thought the benefit of it was that it gave you a certain confidence."

"I have confidence."

"I know you do. I wasn't saying you specifically..."

Sam has chosen not to go to college at this point. After his high school experience, I have to agree with him—although the idea of his being at loose ends frightens me. My question has always been, "OK, but what do you do come Monday morning?"

Sam has followed in the family business and begun to act, and has already achieved some success. I swore that I didn't want any of my children to become actors, but with two in the business, I can only throw my hands up. But if I'm honest with myself, acting saved my life at fifteen. Having been cut by the basketball team, I was aimless when my mother suggested I try out for the school musical. Reluctantly, I did. Surprising myself, I fought for the part. Opening night, I walked out onstage and deep into myself. I never looked back. Who am I to say that acting might not similarly save my kids?

I'm pleased to hear Sam talk of stepping into the world with passion and ambition. "But," I caution, "you have to be careful of your motivations. You want to make sure that the 'proving yourself' is in service of what you want to achieve and not some kind of overassertion to serve your ego. Going past yourself like that, it can get you into trouble."

"You mean don't just try and get famous so you can get laid?" Sam says.

"Good talk, Sam."

Crossing over the Río Porma, on the outskirts of Puente Villarente, we come upon Roger, he of the taxi rides, whom we met the day before. He takes up with us, and we cross over the N-601 and then under the busy A-60 highway. Roger—who appears to be in his late forties—says he's having trouble with his knee but shows no sign of it. He also seems to be well informed on all the gossip that has somehow eluded Sam and me as we naively walked toward Santiago. Apparently, there's an Italian who may or may not be in the Mafia who simply appears in each town. No one has ever seen him walking the trail. This fascinates Roger.

"Is he lying low? Looking for someone? What's his agenda?"

I shake my head, not sure if these questions are rhetorical or not.

Roger is also very invested in someone named Alex from Sri Lanka, who has begun an affair with an American woman whose boyfriend is coming to meet her in León tonight to propose marriage. There is more to this story, but as Roger is discreet, he'll say nothing further about it. He mentions a few other people and situations we're unaware of, but most important, Roger is interested in the motivations people have for walking the Camino.

"There's the reason people tell everyone, and then there's the real reason, the secret reason. Don't ask me mine. I'm not saying."

I shrug—duly warned. I look over at Sam; he seems more concerned with lighting a cigarette without breaking stride.

We all live in bubbles of our own emotional creation that insulate us to one degree or another from clear-eyed reality. Roger's appears more opaque than most.

In the village of Arcahueja, we follow a small, hand-painted sign to a bar tucked off in a side street. While Roger goes to the bathroom, I order some eggs, Sam grabs a Coke and ice cream, and we sit outside. Then Sam calls out, "James!"

We haven't seen our friend in days. Unmistakable in his long cloak, narrow-brimmed hat with feather, and long staff, he sits down. Roger reappears, asking me for help in ordering his food in the local language.

"How have you been eating up to now?" Sam asks.

Roger ignores the question while James grows distracted, then quickly hurries off.

Recrossing over the highway on a massive blue pedestrian bridge built for the safety of pilgrims, we see León, now visible in the valley ahead. Roger mentions his ex-wife, and that his girlfriend is traveling around Spain and will meet him for the last week of walking. He and Sam engage in a spirited discussion of social media, Roger going on at length about his reach and engagement. Sam quizzes him on certain aspects that go over my Luddite head, and I can tell Sam is too gracious to contradict or challenge Roger.

Then, "Do you mind if I ask you a personal question?" Sam asks.

"That depends," Roger warns.

"When did you know your marriage was over? How long before you left it?"

Roger thinks. "Fifteen years."

Sam nods.

After the distressing meltdown I had coming into Burgos, when I couldn't locate the trail by the river, I'm in command of myself walking into León, a city of 130,000. Begun as a Roman military garrison in 74 AD, conquered by Visigoths in 585, taken by the Moors in 712, it was finally reconquered by Christian forces in 853. León wears its history loosely and, unlike many cities, provides an easy welcome. Undisturbed by the confusing and precarious encounters with traffic, we emerge easily into city street-life. The warren of narrow lanes lead to the Santa Maria de León Cathedral, and there is the undeniable feeling of excitement that we are making progress.

"We are definitely getting somewhere, Sammy."

Sam feels it too. "Yeah, bro."

"Pizza?"

"Yeah, bro."

We invite Roger to join us, and the three of us take a seat on the patio outside a restaurant looking up at the thirteenth-century cathedral directly across the plaza. Because it was built in record-setting time of less than a hundred years, the church was done entirely in the

Gothic style, unlike so many other houses of worship along The Way, which evolved over centuries and were subjected to differing architectural moods. And whereas so many Spanish churches were designed to keep the light out, with nearly twenty thousand square feet of stained glass, light is the dominant feature of Santa María, with the goal—as the Cathedral's audio-guide proclaims—of "radiating awesome sacredness." With the main entrance of the cathedral pointing east, the rising sun through the giant windows "creates a celestial celebration."

And celebration feels like the order of the day.

After Roger gets up to go find his hotel, Sam and I order another Coke and sit.

"It's good we're walking and talking about everything," Sam says. "I don't want to be staying in something for fifteen years after I know I shouldn't."

The apartment I rented for the night looks up at the back of the Cathedral, and on our way there we meet Erika, the sad-eyed Hungarian widow. She looks showered and fresh. As her feet are still bothering her, she took a cab into town. I've never seen Erika not by Ryan's side, and at first I take the tall, thin man with her to be him. Instead, he is a German pilgrim. She seems embarrassed to introduce us.

Then in short order, we do come upon Ryan. He's sitting with Chris not far off on a bench outside the Cathedral. Each is writing in a journal.

"Hey, we just saw your friend, Erika," I say.

Ryan nods, a thin smile on his face.

"She was with some German dude," Sam says.

"Oh, good," Ryan says. He's clearly relieved to hear this—that she has found another companion to watch over her. We agree to meet up for dinner and head off.

"Dad, were Ryan and her a couple?"

"Apparently," I say, shaking my head. "I'm oblivious."

"Well, she's certainly got a type, doesn't she?" Sam says.

Dinner is at an outdoor café beside the Cathedral. Ryan and Chris are already seated with the wholesome American couple with the oh-so-bright teeth who took the *Weekend at Bernie's* themed picture with me back outside Burgos. Sam has taken to calling them "The White People." Also at the table is a small and thin bald man with an English accent. He is seated beside a pale-skinned, blond American woman with a glassy look in her eye. This is the couple that Roger told us about—Alex from Sri Lanka and Morgan, who are having the affair. Seated on the other side of Morgan is a burly American with an eager expression, whom we've never seen before. This is, no doubt, Morgan's boyfriend, the man who has come to León today from America to propose. Sam shoots me a quick "oh-this-should-be-good" look and we reach for a table. As we pull it over to join the others, the waiter tells us, "No, no. No possible." James arrives with Roger. They are already quite drunk and pull another table over. The waiter comes by again to assure us this kind of behavior is not permitted. Everyone shouts him down with playful scolding. He throws up his hands and storms off. James tutors Sam in hand-rolling cigarettes. I keep my eyes on the love triangle. Morgan gets up to leave the table, followed soon after by Alex. More people arrive and more tables are pushed together. Morgan's boyfriend is craning his neck looking for his hopefully-soon-to-be fiancée. Food arrives. When Morgan and Alex return to the table, first one and then the other in a not-very-expert attempt to appear as if they were not just off making out in the bathroom together, the boyfriend looks confused. Wine is drunk, talk is loud, and a plan is hatched for everyone to go to the apartment that Alex has rented for the night.

Enough cash is thrown down on the table to pacify the disgruntled waiter who, upon counting it, begins to shake all our hands. Just a half block away, we come upon a large group of Spanish and Italian pilgrims familiar from the trail. The idea of Alex's apartment is aborted and everyone, now totaling more than thirty, descends on a bar down a narrow pedestrian lane in the Barrio Húmedo. Spilling out into the street, it is a Spanish-style party now. Drinks and talk and singing, hugging and shoving. James buys Sam a few shots of some mysterious liquor, and James and I conclude that he is a "wonderfully bad influence" on my son. Sam does one-legged pistol squats with Chris in the street. He bums smokes from a few Spaniards. At one point, someone pulls out a camera, and the entire group smashes together for a photo. It's a raucous, high-spirited mess of a night.

Sam has been swallowed up into the heart of the pulsating group, and I drift off. We have slowly, organically incorporated other pilgrims into our world and find ourselves now a part of a larger, free-forming, ever-shifting whole. For tonight, I'm content to let the group hold my son as he pushes his boundaries. Just away from the bar district, the streets are quiet, the air is soft. I'm satisfied to be alone, my interest in what's around the next corner. Tomorrow, Sam and I will walk on together.

Part 3

It is solved by walking.

—*attributed to St. Augustine*

"It's significantly better"

194 miles to Santiago

"I have to go to the bathroom," Sam says.

We've been walking less than five minutes.

"Why didn't you go before we left?"

"I did."

"You have a medical issue."

We're passing a small, storefront café. It's not the charmless, functional version so typical in Spain—blaring TV, flashing slot machine, wax paper napkins. This place is painted in bright colors, with intricately woven pillows tossed on benches, filigreed lamps, and smoked mirrors with ornate frames. The man behind the bar is Moroccan, and I order two coffees that neither Sam nor I need, since we just drank the ones I brought back to our room less than a half hour earlier. Sam hurries to the toilet.

I compliment the man on his café. He's pleased and places small pieces of toast topped with a tomato spread down in front of me.

"We don't get many pilgrims in here," he says.

Perhaps because we're generally a dirty and smelly lot, most pilgrims tend to frequent cheap and utilitarian spots along the way.

"Well, that's their loss," I tell my generous host.

Sam emerges from the bathroom. "What's this?" he asks, nodding toward the toast with the red spread on it.

"Try it."

"Wow, that's good." He sips his black coffee. "And that's excellent coffee."

Such pauses as this one, trivial and inconsequential in isolation, gain meaning in the aggregate and fill the journey with significance not always obvious in the moment.

Crossing the Plaza San Marcos, we pass the twelfth-century monastery and pilgrims' hospital that years ago became a five-star hotel. I have a distinct memory of a lonely stay there on my last journey. Like this time, I had begun to make friends on the trail by this stage, but instead of staying close with them, I isolated myself behind these gilded walls. I felt the separation keenly that night. I've not forgotten. As we pass the Renaissance facade, Sam says, "I'm really getting used to the black coffee thing. That coffee was delicious."

"Well, he put a ton of sugar in it."

"He did?"

I shrug. "He's Moroccan."

Across the Río Bernesga, through more contemporary and ugly outskirts, past housing developments, warehouses and trucks, across highway overpasses and under electrical wires, past homes dug into the earth that Sam has taken to calling "Hobbit houses," it takes us a few hours to clear the city. During this time, Sam accuses me of being sentimental, while I insist it's just emotional availability. "I don't know, Dad, you start crying over..." And he shrugs. We engage in a long and pointless discussion on the hypothetical pleasure of driving a Corvette vs. the cringe factor involved. "I've only driven one once," I tell Sam. "I was in L.A., and one night I was out with Bob Seger and guys in his band, randomly enough."

"Who's he?"

"He was a big rock star back in the day. Still is, to people like me."

"You were kind of hot shit back then, huh?"

"Well, there was a moment, Sammy. But I somehow didn't even know it at the time."

"You're so weird."

"Yeah, anyway, we got pulled over. I was flying down the road, half drunk. When the cop sees Bob Seger next to me, he let us go." I laugh at the memory. "It was a different time. Anyway, this is a cautionary tale and not a story to be admired or imitated," I say with little conviction.

When Sam eventually talks of The Ex, it feels somehow more a part of the past in a way that it hasn't up to now.

Just beyond the suburban spread of La Virgen del Camino, the path splits. The two divergent trails meet up again halfway into tomorrow's walk. The traditional route tracks the busy, ugly N-120 highway. We slip off down a dirt lane along the alternate route.

"This trail must be longer if it's the way we're going," Sam says.

"It is. Plus I couldn't find us a room in the other village."

Soon we're walking beside an abandoned road and, an hour later, we come upon a bar with tables out in the shade.

After his most recent success with black coffee leaving León, Sam eagerly orders another. The young woman behind the counter is quick to help. We take a seat outside. The coffee arrives. Sam raises the cup and drinks. He purses his lips.

"It's significantly better with sugar."

"Most things are."

"Shit."

"One step up and two steps back, Sammy."

As we're leaving, Alex from Sri Lanka arrives in his yellow Hawaiian shirt and floppy hat, accompanied by a friend named Felix, who has flown in from England to join the walk for a few days. Morgan is nowhere in sight.

Alex takes the initiative. "How'd you enjoy the party last night, gentlemen?" he asks. There's a smirk on his face.

"Yeah, it was fun," I say. "You have a good time?" There's probably a smirk on my face too.

Sam is more direct and asks where Morgan is.

"We're on the alternate route, here," Alex informs us, as if this is an explanation. While solicitous in a well-bred manner, he displays the smug satisfaction of a man chuffed to be fucking another man's woman.

Once we're walking again, Sam asks, "What do you think is gonna happen with Alex and Morgan?"

"That could go in any number of directions," I say. "All I know is I'm glad I'm not in her shoes today."

"What do you think of Alex?"

"He's fine, I guess."

We're on a dirt track now, but unlike nearly the entire Camino, the land we walk through has not been cultivated. Long brown grass grows wild; trees appear in clusters. Hills roll and rise and fall. The lack of organization in the land is disconcerting. A fox darts across our path and disappears into the long grass.

We discuss the mindset of scarcity vs. abundance. Sam is thinking about this in regard to sex. "Now that I'm single..." He shrugs.

"I think you'll be all right."

"But, Dad"—Sam has a gleam in his eye—"to be Chad is the manifestation of the divine masculine." Over the course of the walk, I've become fairly adept at translating Samspeak—in this case, to be a stud is to be a real man.

"Please stop talking, Sam."

"What?" There's a disingenuous quality to his feigned ignorance.

"Don't be a pig. You're sounding like Alex."

"Well, he's definitely not Chad."

"No, but at this moment he'd like to believe he is."

The village of Oncina de la Valdoncina is lifeless and deserted in midafternoon. We look briefly for a place to stop, but find nothing open. A small, white delivery van races past us and screeches to a stop. A man hurries out, grabs a loaf of bread from the back of his van, and scurries up to a deserted-looking house. He knocks with impatience and, in time, an old woman opens the door a crack. The man shoves the bread into her hand, and the door slams shut. Then he's down the stoop and back in his van, screeching away. I feel like I've just witnessed a drug deal instead of a bread delivery. A hundred yards down the road, at a similarly deserted-looking home, the action repeats itself.

For the next six miles, until our destination of Villar de Mazarife, the path is dirt, through rich-looking soil. Fields have been tilled and await the fall crop. Others have been shorn of their wheat. Order has returned to the landscape. Sam races ahead for the final haul of the day.

As he does, I begin to experience a shooting pain in my left shin. The lingering blisters on my toes now rub and burn. The afternoon heat is up again, the sun is strong. The pain in my shin, seemingly from nowhere, intensifies. I'm limping now. I conclude that I must have a stress fracture—whatever that is.

The woman behind the bar at Tio Pepe is in her thirties, with straight, peroxide-blond hair. She wears a tight, black Guns N' Roses T-shirt. Her teeth are bleached the color of her skintight pants—we are suddenly in the East Village of Manhattan in the 1990s.

When I inform her that we have a reservation at the albergue for the night, she flashes those shimmering teeth at me and points down the bar to a short, round man in his sixties with sun-creased skin and a drooping mustache—and we are back in rural Spain. Pepe nods and silently leads us through the bar and then a courtyard to where we will sleep.

Dropping his pack, Sam says, "I'm gonna get an ice cream and say hi to the White People."

"Are they here?" I ask, collapsing on the bed and swinging my feet up the wall.

"We just walked right by them, at a table in the courtyard. They said 'hi.'"

"Oh, OK. I'll be down. My shin is really killing me, I don't know what happened. I might have a stress fracture or something. But I've got a lot of pain."

"All right, whatever."

Hanging on the wall beside my upwardly extended feet is a poster in the form of a large postcard. On it is a drawing of the U.S. Capitol with the words 'New York City' scrawled at a jaunty angle. Staring at this incongruity, I consider Sam's complete lack of concern for my condition. It speaks to the parent/child dynamic in which I as the parent take care of my child's needs, and being the parent, have no needs of my own. It might also speak to the part of me that has kept my needs aloof from my son, choosing only the emotional safety of that parent/child relationship, so that now when empathy is needed on his part, there is no habit-life of concern to call upon. Or maybe Sam's cavalier "man-up" attitude is appropriate, and I just need to stop acting like a baby.

Both my guidebooks claim that Villar de Mazarife is a "decidedly friendly pilgrim town." Perhaps, but there is so little life on the street that I can't confirm this. It seems to me, like all the villages along this "alternate" route today, more of a ghost town. The mud-and-brick church is humble and empty. The few contraptions in the spartan playground sit idle and rusting. The one local market is appropriately called "Frutas de Camino de Santiago." I am the sole customer and attempt to buy two peaches for the trail tomorrow. The woman behind the register calls someone to get the price. This process takes time. Not only does the woman behind the register get the price of the peaches, but of each fruit and vegetable in the store. I wait and watch as she writes it all down on a scrap of paper.

Back in the courtyard of Tio Pepe, Sam is seated with Hallie and Duncan—The White People. They have been joined by Alex and his friend Felix. Morgan is also there now, the tips of her fingers intertwined with Alex's.

"I thought you were on the other path today," I say politically, by way of greeting.

"I was." She smiles sheepishly. "I changed."

"Horses in midstream?"

"Something like that."

I nod and take a seat at the large table.

One of the pleasures of a lifeless place like Mazarife is that so little is going on by way of enticement or distraction that pilgrims tend to create their own entertainment, which generally entails sitting in one spot and talking. Hours drift by, bad food is served and eaten, drinks are drunk.

The White People are, as usual, discussing their impending wedding in Costa Rica. They invite all assembled who choose to make their own way to Central America to attend the celebration. Sam huddles at one end of the table with Alex. They smoke. From the snippets of conversation I hear, Sam is sharing, honestly and clearly, the processing of his relationship. Alex, for his part, offers pronouncements.

I turn to Morgan.

"So," I begin, hoping that my manner—while direct—is both playful and empathetic, "what the hell is going on with you?"

Other conversations around the table fade. All eyes turn to Morgan, who seems both relieved by the question and eager to share. Her boyfriend did in fact come to propose marriage. Instead of accepting, she broke up with him on the trail today. She then forged her way off-map to this alternate path, and here she is, with Alex. A graduate psychology student, the most organized, anal, responsible person she knows, nothing like this has ever happened to her in her life. "I have no idea what I am doing," Morgan confesses. "I don't recognize myself at all."

The human simplicity of her assessment causes me to apologize in my mind for my earlier silent judgment. Affection and good wishes replace my self-satisfied and superior assessment. What I see now is a lovely young woman, just trying to work it out, like the rest of us.

"I am having an existential crisis," Morgan concludes.

"Maybe," I say.

"Or maybe the Camino is just doing its thing," Sam adds from down the table.

"The ultimate in cool"

182 miles to Santiago

The deserted country lane we're walking down is pointing dead west, and our striding shadows stretch out before us. In the distance rise the Montes de León. They are a concern for a few days from now, but this morning the land is flat. We're flanked by well-irrigated cornfields and come upon a lone car just off the road. It's at an awkward angle, as if parked in a hurry. Its trunk is flung open. A man emerges from the high corn carrying a shovel. He's startled to see us, mutters a quick, *"Buen Camino,"* and turns away.

We nod in return and walk on in silence. When we're out of earshot I turn to Sam. "I think I've seen too many Coen brothers movies, but that seems like a perfect place to dispose of a body."

"I was thinking that too."

My blisters are abating, and my leg today is magically much improved.

"So it's not a stress fracture after all?" Sam says.

I ignore his sarcastic tone and thank him for his concern.

We pass a marker—"300 km" to Santiago. These signs tend to be inconsistent at best. We're just as likely to come upon one in a few miles telling us we are at "312 km" as we are one that might read "284 km." Such signposts provide momentary distraction and can be a source of amusement or frustration, depending on mood. We pass a canal and cross railroad tracks. A handful of swallows darts overhead.

"Do you think birds like flying?" Sam asks.

"I hope so," I say.

ANDREW MCCARTHY

Leading into the town of Hospital de Órbigo is a long, thirteenth-century, many-arched Gothic bridge. It was here, in 1434, that Don Suero de Quiñones regained his honor. The noble knight had been scorned and humiliated in love. Word went forth far and wide that in order to recapture his dignity, Don Suero would joust and defeat three hundred challengers. And so he did. Self-respect restored, he marched to Santiago, where the bejeweled iron collar he wore during his heroic deed can still be seen in the Cathedral Museum.

While Sam's yoke may not be iron or covered in precious gems, he has been working hard along The Way to reestablish his own sense of dignity. In a fine example of Samspeak, he offers a realization as we step out onto the cobbled bridge. "The more ambrosia you put on, the less cool you are."

"I think the word you were looking for was maybe affectation, not ambrosia?"

"Don't be so literal, bro."

"Sorry."

"Just being yourself is cool." There's no denying that Sam has a jump in his step as we cross the bridge. "And knowing you're cool in yourself, that's the ultimate in cool."

Trying on different personalities is a natural part of adolescence, and Sam has been no exception—the music, the mirror, the privacy, the germs, the baggy clothes, the tight clothes, the lingo—but the sense of devastation and feelings of being lost with which he began this trek were real. To see him coming home to himself is both attractive and satisfying. I smile at my son.

"What?"

"Nothing," I say. "Sounding good."

Not much farther along, after the hamlet of Villares de Órbigo, we begin to see rolling hills again. The monotony of the Meseta, while maddening, was consistent, and the loss of such predictability causes a flutter of anxiety as well as a twinge of excitement. Sam walks ahead as we pass groves of holm oak and occasional orchards. The path is wide and dirt now.

With the solitary repetition of step after step after step after step, my mind begins to indulge in a strange waking dream. I'm dying. I'm not sure if I'm in a hospital or exactly where I am. I am surrounded by my wife and children. They are all touching me lightly, on my arms, my torso, my legs, whatever part of me is closest to where they stand over me. As I am taking my last breaths, I say simply, "It's beautiful. It's beautiful." Am I speaking about the love that envelops me or of what lies beyond the threshold I am about to pass over? The depth of joy contained in those few words is beyond my understanding.

It does not take moments as oddly wondrous or peculiar as this to make the Camino I am walking unique from the Camino anyone else is walking—unique even from that of Sam, who for most of the way is stride for stride beside me. Such unlikely reveries as my waking dream aside, the mere whims of mood can inform our experiences to such a degree as to make them all but unrecognizable compared to the experiences of others. In the morning, the steep hill might be an invigorating wake-up, while in the weary afternoon the same trudge could prove almost insurmountable. The surly waiter at lunch might be irritating, but in the satisfaction of the evening, I may find him amusing. Our internal caprices create our individual experiences as much or more than the country we cross or the people we encounter.

This is, of course, true in so many areas of life—but I first grew aware of it as it relates to the Camino. Not long after my first walk across Spain, a German woman with whom I had become friends while on the trail was visiting New York and we got together to reminisce. She had with her a friend from Toronto whom I had also known from Spain—but only peripherally. He had brought along photographs of his walk. Although we had been moving over the same land on the exact same days, other than obvious landmarks, nothing in his photos looked familiar or reminded me of my journey in any way. His stories and recollections were completely alien to me. Hiking the same road at the same time, we might as well have been in parallel universes. We had each walked, as everyone does, a very personal path. This sentiment is brought home to me when I come upon Sam sitting at what might best be described as an oasis, staring off in his own private and pensive mood.

By the side of a lonely stretch of the trail, a large round harvest table has been laid with a bounty of fruit: watermelon and bananas, kiwi, peaches, plums and apples. There are walnuts and olives, and a bowl of oranges sits beside a long knife and an industrial-looking squeezer. A carved wooden box sits on the table for donations. Nearby, in the shade of a few trees, hammocks have been strung up. A man I don't recognize, wearing long hair and a tie-dyed shirt, is standing nearby watching. I assume this is all his doing.

"Wow," I say.

He nods, and I take a seat.

Sam, seated on the other side of the table, is shirtless and appears dehydrated. I urge watermelon on him. It's sweet and dripping. The long-haired man grabs a backpack I hadn't noticed, hoists it, and sets off down the trail.

"Oh," I say to Sam, "I thought this was his place."

Sam grunts a response and stares off.

"Have some more watermelon," I tell him. "It's so sweet."

He doesn't move, and I put a piece in his hand. "Thanks," he mutters.

After several minutes watching birds peck at the ground, I'm ready to move on, but I can see Sam needs more time. No sooner have I returned my attention to the birds than Sam jumps up and grabs his pack. Before it's even halfway on, he's calling over his shoulder, "I'll see you there," and he bolts off down the trail.

I reach for my rucksack, but Sam is gone, racing away. I resent his dismissal and grow angry. For the next hour, I walk past plowed fields and rows of planted pines, my anger stewing. A goshawk flies low overhead, the cinnamon-brown striping of its underbelly and barred tail in evidence. It's impossible for me to see one and not think of a painting that hung in our home growing up. It was a medium-large canvas depicting of the head of a goshawk in profile—its yellow/orange eyes, its supercilia, its hooked beak. Something about the depiction of simultaneous strength and delicacy always captured my attention. I loved the painting. No one else in my family seemed to ever notice it, and I don't recall it ever being mentioned. It was just there. As I was getting ready to leave for college, I asked my mother if I could have it. She agreed. When my father saw the painting off the wall and propped beside the back door, then heard it was accompanying me to New York, he grew enraged.

"That is my favorite painting!" he bellowed. "That is not leaving this house." I quickly acquiesced, but my mother, in an unlikely move, stood her ground. "Andrew asked for it. I bought it, and if he wants it, he can have it." A horrific hour ensued. In the end, my father dismissed the painting (and me, I felt) with a backhanded wave. "Take it," he hissed.

I no longer wanted the painting, but my father now insisted I have it. It was shoved into the car and accompanied me across the river to the city, where I crammed it into the back of the closet in my apartment off Washington Square. When I moved on a year later, I left without it.

"All that anger," I say aloud now to no one. "For what purpose?" I walk on.

I come upon Sam waiting for me on the outskirts of a town called San Justo de la Vega.

"Sorry, Dad."

"You're good, Sammy. It's hot."

It takes us another hour, over a massive, taxpayer-funded, ramped maze of a footbridge spanning the railroad tracks and then up a steep incline, to be deposited inside the medieval walls and into the muscular mini-metropolis of Astorga, home to twelve thousand souls. Legend decrees that both Saint James and Saint Paul preached here. Saint Francis slept here on the way to Santiago in 1214. (St. Francis along the Camino is not unlike George Washington throughout the Northeast of America; he seems to have slept everywhere.) The site of convergence for several ancient Roman trails, Astorga still retains the energy of a bustling market town. Beside the fifteenth-century cathedral is Gaudí's Palacio Episcopal, a neo-Gothic fairytale of a place that today houses a museum dedicated in large part to the Camino. Inside are statues and carvings of its patron saint through the ages. Seeing them all clustered together, I'm reminded of how James has been co-opted to suit the preferred message of the day. There is James the warrior, atop a handsome steed and wielding a long sword; James the humble, kneeling in supplication; James the pilgrim, striding in long cloak and staff; and James the devout, standing simply, reading from a bible.

Our own James of the straw hat, the rakish, ne'er-do-well, bad influence on my son, and all-around delight, joins Sam and myself, as well as The Boys, The White People, Morgan and Alex and his friend Felix, and Roger, whom Sam has recently dubbed Taxicab Roger. We're all crowded around a few outdoor tables at a café in the Plaza Mayor. Over my shoulder, the clock atop the Ayuntamiento clangs out the hour. Two mechanical figures dressed in black costumes of the local Maragato people strike the bell with hammers, the thin sound echoing across the misshapen square. There was no plan for us all to meet, but by now everyone in our motley crew gravitates like migrating animals that instinctively know where to be and when. The drinks and meal and comings and goings create the usual frustrations for the eventually overtipped waiter. Multiple conversations overlap and fade; shouted interruptions are made. There is laughter. But around the table tonight, the group appears tired. The walk is long, and there are days when the accumulation of distance under extreme conditions is evident. I make an early exit, leaving Sam to talk with Chris about their walking to Finisterre together. Roger follows me off, and we make a fruitless search for gelato. Looking up at the Gaudí Palace one last time in the late gloaming, it occurs to me that today was the first day of the entire trip that Sam did not mention The Ex.

"Sky Daddy has a plan"

163 miles to Santiago

I'm falling. Fast. Because I'm carrying an added twenty-plus pounds on my back, I'm falling with more propulsion than I would normally fall. It feels like I'm in someone else's body, or that some cruel and unseen hand is shoving me down with malicious intent. My face goes rushing past the hip-high cement obelisk that we're passing at this instant. I miss it by inches. I land hard on the ground.

"Dad!" Sam screams.

"It's OK," I gasp.

I tend to be pretty agile; I have excellent spatial awareness. I don't usually stumble and rarely fall. If for no other reason than I am so mortified when I do, I'm conscious of my surroundings in order to prevent such a humiliation. And on the odd occasion when I do take a spill, my tendency is to bounce back on my feet instantly in order to dispel unwanted and embarrassing attention. This time I stay down. My current vulnerability lets me know just how taxing this walk is on me, how few reserves I have when something beyond what is needed for the task at hand is called upon.

"Whoa," I say. Still on the ground. I'm shaken.

"Are you all right?" Sam bends down to me.

"Yeah," I pant.

"Jesus, you're lucky you missed that cement thing."

A horrifying image of smashing into the obelisk races into my mind. Had I hit it, my jaw might have shattered, or my head concussed. It's age that brings an awareness of the luck of life, how the tiniest membrane can be the difference between a calamity causing enduring hardship and the near miss that allows us to press on, clinging to delusions of invincibility, with the potentially catastrophic incident soon forgotten.

I don't know that Sam has ever seen me so out of physical control. I feel utterly exposed in this instant. I don't want my son to see me so unsteady, so vulnerable. But this too is part of what I have to offer him— not only the times when he views me as perceptive or skilled or even wise. Maybe moments like this are more valuable for him to witness. My human frailty.

He helps me to my feet.

"Thanks, Sammy."

We had been walking over a narrow trail outside the village of Murias de Rechivaldo. Sam and I were in the midst of a discussion on space travel when, walking side by side, the trail narrowed to be only wide enough for a single walker. I had slowed to let Sam step ahead, but as single-file walking discourages talk, and I was eager to continue our conversation, I stepped slightly off the trail to regain him. As I walked through the wispy weeds, Sam went on. "I'd basically give up my entire existence to experience another planet."

Just ahead was one of the cement mile markers announcing the distance remaining to Santiago, in this case, "272 km." As we came upon the waist-high obelisk, I began to step around it. It was then that I tripped on the unseen root and went down, narrowly missing a collision with the pylon.

The morning had begun in the usual fashion, with me draining and taping blisters and applying ointment, while intermittently calling out to the lump in the bed beside me.

Out the hotel window, I noticed James with his hat and jaunty feather, filling his water bottle at a fountain in front of the Gaudí Palace, then strutting on. For some reason, the sight filled me with pride and an affection for him.

Once we were out the door, Sam was taken with the ornate facade of Astorga's Cathedral—his first exposure to a full-blown example of Baroque architecture. It was also the first time Sam had paid any attention to any church along The Way.

"Where'd all the money come from?" Sam asked, almost rhetorically. This led us into a spirited discussion of the Catholic Church's financial practices. "Why do you think priests can't get married?" I asked. "Because the Church didn't want to give up its property."

"I thought it was supposed to be like marrying God or something."

"That's nuns, but it's basically the same story."

I railed about the horrific sexual abuses disclosed in recent decades. While I was vehement in my outrage, Sam bypassed my repulsion and left the church to its own devices.

"I'm a nihilistic optimist," he said. "I like that better than, 'Sky Daddy has a plan.'"

Sam then began speaking of Alan Watts.

"Who's he?"

"Remember, I played you a talk of his, with the spacey music?"

Conversation evolved into the idea of just what the hell we're doing here and is any of it even real.

"I mean, even if we're an alien simulation or a computer rendering, it makes no difference to day-to-day life. So it's cool." Sam went on. "Or we're all part of some collective consciousness."

"Really?"

"Well, when I did acid, I saw the collective consciousness. It was a blue cloud with little fingers."

I let that slide past without reaction.

Sam went on about the time/space continuum and then free will, and I began to wonder when it is along the way that children start to develop their own theories of life and existence.

"Where'd you learn all this stuff?"

"YouTube."

And that's when things evolved to talk of space travel, and we came upon the cement mile marker, and I tripped and fell.

No one is sure who, exactly, the Maragato people are or from where they originated, and this includes the Maragato themselves. They may date back to the seventh century, when King Mauregato and the Visigoths became isolated in this remote section of Spain during the Arab invasion. Some say they descended from Berber tribes who came in the eighth century. It's generally agreed that they were mule drivers who transported food and gold. The few remaining Maragato strive to retain their culture of cuisine and dress, but nothing has done as much to revive these forty or so ghost towns surrounding Astorga than the resurgence of the Camino. Sam and I pass through Castrillo de los Polvazares and Santa Catalina de Somoza and the crumbling town of El Ganso, all characterized by stone dwellings with thatch or slate roofs. The incongruity of a Tex-Mex establishment called Meson Cowboy adds to the displaced, eerie quality of El Ganso, and we stop for a drink. No one ever appears to serve us, and in time we move on.

As we leave the decaying village quickly behind, the trail takes us up the side of the seldom-used LE-142 road. As is often the case in the afternoon, Sam plugs in his earbuds and charges ahead. He's running, shirt off, singing along to his music, his pack bouncing up and down as he veers off into the center of the road. I call for him to move back to the trail, but he can't hear me. He's juking left, then right, as he dance-struts down the middle of the road and disappears over the rise. I call out again, but he's gone from view. I hear a car approaching over my shoulder. A white van is closing fast. I step out into the road, frantically waving my stick. The van swerves around me without slowing. I start to run, following, screaming. Sam's back becomes just visible over the rise. He's slightly over the median, in the oncoming lane. The van doesn't slow. Sam can't hear it closing in. He begins to juke and jive again, dancing first left and then right again, crossing back over the center of the road. The van is almost upon him. Sam shimmies left, and as he leaps right, the van swerves hard. When it races past, inches from him, Sam whips around. He sees me running, waving, shouting. He takes his earbud out.

"GET THE FUCK OUT OF THE ROAD!" I scream.

Sam shrugs and complies.

I am glad he is a few hundred yards ahead of me. Nothing good could come from what I have to say to him right now.

The trail narrows and enters a wooded area of birch and maple and holly, and the afternoon sun dapples the ground. The meandering path climbs. The trail is as bucolic as I am agitated. In time the terrain pacifies me, and I relax into a harmonious hour of solitary walking.

No Maragato village has benefitted more from the resurgence of the Camino than Rabanal. Its stone buildings along Calle Real are finely repointed and camera ready. Pilgrim trade has given this town purpose, and Rabanal has repaid the walker with welcoming services and restored churches. Sam is waiting at an outdoor café with inviting umbrellas. We order gazpacho and a plate of jamón serrano as a half dozen vultures circle above.

"Almost got yourself killed back there, huh, Sammy?" I say casually.

He drops his head. "Yeah."

The trail keeps climbing through more maple and holly; the sun still shines down. A breeze kicks up and leaves blow, shadows dance on the snaking trail. The air begins to turn cooler. Two strenuous and satisfying hours later, we break through the tree line to the village of Foncebadón. The Maragato settlement is a string of a dozen stone houses and that many ruins draped along a road that keeps to a steady incline. If it were not for the Camino, this hamlet would no longer exist. It is on the way to nowhere. Fog rolls down the mountain, the air is chilled. We see Taxicab

Roger, fresh from a day of not walking, and then we come upon The Boys—Ryan and Chris, and The White People. Looking for our lodging, I walk into a beautifully restored stone building to find a family around the dinner table. They all wave hello. I call out a greeting in return and keep coming. They begin to shout, *"Privado! Privado!"* smiles on their faces. I don't understand and keep coming. *"Privado!"* they all call again, laughing now. Then I realize. My hands fly to cover my face. They laugh harder. Embarrassed, I back out of the home through the strands of hanging beads and leave them to their family dinner.

The gang, plus a few others, descend on a small pizza place run by a misplaced Italian. The pizzas are surprisingly good considering we are very far from...anywhere. The evening is cold, and I have put on more layers than I have worn the entire trip. After the meal, Chris and Ryan take Sam and The White People off into a field, and they settle into a circle for some Wim Hof breathing exercises.

Heading back to take the laundry down from the line in the yard of our hostel before bed, I come upon a small child no more than two years old throwing a tantrum in the street. The toddler's mother half-heartedly tries to console him, to no avail. The child flings himself down and begins to roll from side to side on his back on the pavement. The woman watches. In time, she turns and walks away, up the hill, leaving the wailing tot in the middle of the street. The child, for his part, cries harder. I begin to walk away as well, then return and sit not far off by the side of the road. Just being there. A long time passes until the child stops crying enough to get up and trundle up the hill.

"Huh," I say aloud.

"The easiest thing I have ever done"

147 miles to Santiago

Taxicab Roger is disgusted. "I ordered a damn taxi yesterday, and it never came. I waited two hours. I had to order another one, and it took an hour to get there."

"Jeez, you could have almost walked here quicker," I say, shaking my head.

Sam stifles a grin. Roger is nonplussed.

We're standing in the middle of the single lane, not far from where the crying child was last evening, on the road that leads up to Cruz de Ferro. Believed to have been erected by ancient Celts, later co-opted by Romans and dedicated to the god Mercury, then crowned with an iron cross and claimed by ninth-century Christians, the tall wooden pole atop a pile of crumbling stones has become one of the enduring symbols of the Camino. As tradition dictates, Sam and I each selected a rock from home, placed them in our packs, and have carried them across Spain to deposit at the base of the cross—a symbol of a specific burden we've carried in life and would like to leave behind.

This is one of the few Camino traditions that Sam has shown an interest in, and he turns to Roger.

"I heard you have seven stones to leave at the cross thing."

"More like nine," Roger says.

"Nine!" I say. "No wonder you're taking cabs."

"It's my knee," Roger assures me. "But I'm gonna walk up to the cross and drop my stones and then come back down and take a cab to Ponferrada."

"See you there, Roger," I say, as Sam and I turn uphill. It's cold as we lean into the steep grade. A crumbling ruin of a ninth-century pilgrim's hospital is just off the dirt path. Wind whips down the mountain; the rising sun behind us in the valley below offers no warmth yet.

"Fuck, I'm freezing," Sam barks.

Less than a mile up the winding path, we come upon the thirty-foot pole buried into a pile of rocks nearly as high. We drop our packs and dig out our small stones. I tend not to give much credence to rituals such as these, but I say a quick prayer and toss my burden down. Sam stomps up the mound, raps the pole, and stands like a conquering hero astride the hill.

The narrow and uneven trail continues to climb and then dips and climbs again, through purple flowering heather and long golden grass and past rowan trees heavy with orange and red berries. At the crest of the rise, just under five thousand feet, and the highest point on the Camino de Santiago, we can make out motionless windmills on distant peaks. Far ahead, beyond rolling hills, deep down in the valley, the large town of Ponferrada is visible.

"Oh my God," I say. "Look how far that is."

"This is literally the easiest thing I have ever done in my life," Sam scoffs, and the trail begins to plunge.

Sam tries to convince me that cut-off jeans, what he calls, "jorts," are a cool thing.

"I'm sorry, Sam. You've been in the sun too long. There is nothing cool about jorts. Even the name..."

"No, bro. You're wrong." This ridiculous back-and-forth goes on for far too long. Then we talk skydiving—Sam can't wait to try it. I never will. And tattoos. During much of his teen years, Sam tried to convince me that he should get a tattoo. My own skin is unmarked by body art, and I told him he would have to wait until he was eighteen. Since attaining legal age, he has resisted the impulse, but is once again considering the idea. I try to convince him that in later life the glorious design on his taut and shredded arms may not age well, what with fading, sagging, wrinkling, and the like.

"Yeah," Sam agrees, "all is well and cool till you're thirty-five, then..."

"I was actually thinking more like sixty-five."

In the mountain village of El Acebo, we stop at an attractive café with patio seating beside the twisting, descending road. The dark-haired man who takes our order speaks Spanish with an American accent.

"Where are you from?" I ask in English.

"Houston," he tells me.

Mike came to Spain twelve years ago on vacation and never left. He'd had enough of the world of finance, and now runs this decidedly Spanish establishment. He also makes us the closet thing we've had in Spain to an American breakfast of fried eggs and bacon (with grilled jamón substituting nicely for American bacon).

While Sam enjoys a dessert of late-morning ice cream, a taxi comes winding down the road.

"That's probably Roger," Sam says.

When the car passes, the man leaning across the back seat waving frantically at us is none other.

I get the bill and chat with Mike, and when Sam doesn't come out of the bathroom for a half hour, I leave him. The Camino travels down the center of this one-road village, past restored stone houses with wooden balconies and wood-shuttered windows flung open. It deposits the walker onto a steep and rocky trail. During one stage of treacherous switchbacks, Sam races past me with a simple "Yo." I can hear his blaring music bleeding out of his earbuds.

The trail continues its steep decline, through another storybook village of stone houses, then through a magnificent grove of mature chestnut trees. On the valley floor, the stone Puente de los Peregrinos crosses the Río Meruela. I catch up with Sam, and we enter the inviting town of Molinaseca and lay our packs on the expanse of grass beside the river. The water above the bridge has been dammed, creating a swimming area. Chris calls out—he and Ryan are already there and in the water. Sam strips off his shirt and dives in.

Having been cast in the role of the elder statesman on the trip (When did this happen in life?) I live up to character and sit on the edge of a small, stone-lined diversion in the river, cooling my feet in the frigid stream and watching the young'uns swim and the river flow.

Since León, something has happened; the Camino has changed. After the hardscrabble existence along the Meseta, the terrain has become more varied, the weather cooler. But there's been an internal change as well. We have been walking for several weeks now, and the routine of road life has become ingrained. Repetition has become a friend, something to be relied upon; it supports our efforts and pacifies thought. Anxiety has abated. The need to constantly press on has transformed into simple awareness of what needs to be done each day. There is more internal space. I am not the only one feeling this way. The Boys, The White People, James, even Taxicab Roger, are all more relaxed, playful. Perhaps it's the feeling of support that comes from being a part of a loose, ever-shifting, traveling "community" of walkers that creates this feeling of freedom, or maybe it's that so much of the road is behind us and yet we are not so close to the end that thoughts of life beyond the Camino are much more than an optimistic promise to carry the lessons learned here into the everyday world.

A few hours down the trail is Ponferrada, a working town of seventy thousand. Its factories, garbage, grinding traffic—all the typically unpleasant features one finds in the outskirts of a big town—can't help but dampen the spirit, while its attractive medieval town center serves to revive it. I've had good success at selecting, sight unseen, places for us to stay—local places, small and family run whenever possible. It's tougher in the big towns, and today's stop lacks any charm and welcome. But it's situated across from the twelfth-century Templar castle, built on the ruins of a Visigoth fort, which was built over a Roman fort, which was in turn built over an earlier castro. While the Knights Templar created a grand and imposing home for themselves, they didn't enjoy it for long. By 1312, they were outlawed and disbanded.

The castle is too imposing and formal to entice me. I find myself instead sitting in front of the Iglesia de Santa María on a stone bench, staring up its bell tower. A long time passes in which no discernable thoughts cross my mind. Sam is at a café in the Plaza Encina with the gang. When I wander over, James has reappeared after a conspicuous absence. I notice the clear liquid in front of him, instead of his usual red wine. The feather in his hat appears off-kilter. He looks a little worse for the walk.

"Water?"

"Yes, my love. Water."

"I won't ask.

"Best not to."

The group heads off for sushi. While there is satisfaction for both of us in the rhythm of our relationship, as well as rewards and challenges in its occasional intensity, I'm aware how much Sam embraces the camaraderie of the group. He needs and wants more than I have to offer him. That I would rather spend the evening in his company or on my own speaks only to my loner tendencies and is of little consequence compared with what I know my son is getting from the group—and I don't want to miss that.

The Spanish live their nightlife in the streets and cafés and later, strolling back through a buzzing town center, Sam talks of The Ex for the first time in a few days. He speaks with more self-possession, detachment, and perspective than I would have imagined possible when we were crossing the Pyrenees several weeks earlier. Perhaps there is something to the Cruz de Ferro and the laying down of one's burden after all. Maybe Roger was on to something with his nine stones.

"If anyone's killed someone, it's him"

129 miles to Santiago

"I gotta sleep, Dad."

"All right, Sammy." I finish tying my shoes.

"I'm not really gonna sleep more. I just want to get up slow."

"That's fine, kiddo. I'll see you for lunch."

I hear the unmistakable pilgrim call of metal rapping on pavement. Glancing out the window, I see two Germans I recognize walking down the middle of the street, each with ski-poles in either hand, clacking as they go like some kind of spidery hybrid. The nervous sound echoes in the early silence. The morning is cool, the way the mornings have been these past days.

The sun is noticeably later to rise the deeper into the season it gets, and the farther west we go. I pass the Templar Castle and cross over the Río Sil. As has been the case when I walk out solo, I'm happy to be alone, while I'm sad to be without Sam. The paradox of parenthood.

Down by the river, I pass something called the Museum of Energy. Outside it stands a giant brick smokestack rising like the ghost of industry past. I pass under electrical wires and beside a soccer pitch, past parked cars, a lonely playground, then under a highway and by overgrown fields. Is it just suburbia that elicits the emptiness of spirit I feel this morning? There is only the sound of my steps and the rhythmic swaying of my pack. Occasionally, one of my feet scuffs the pavement and, with obsessive-compulsive focus, I try to scrape the other in order to "even" myself out. A cemetery is on my left, a vineyard to my right. The sun finally rises over my shoulder through a thin haze as I pass a small, nearly windowless church.

The suburb of Columbrianos is still shuttered except for two small, gray-haired women. One is wearing a blue apron and holds a broom; the other carries a small shopping bag. They stand in the gutter whispering. To the south, the mountains fade into haze. The tops of the mountains ahead aren't visible for the clouds. The village of O Cebreiro is in those clouds. It's a place I've thought of for twenty-six years. Tomorrow.

Several hours of walking have not taken me away from pavement, and in the long and featureless town of Camponaraya, at a traffic roundabout, I duck into a bar. Dirty dishes are stacked high on the counter. The tired-looking young woman at the sink gives me a cursory glance. Whatever hopes I had for a welcoming breakfast fade with that look—then she smiles. The shroud of emptiness I've worn all morning falls off me on receipt of that smile. My host happily agrees to fry me some eggs after making me a frothy café con leche. Sitting at a table outside, inhaling the fumes of cars chasing through the roundabout, I satisfy my hunger and order another coffee. My mood is rising by the minute.

Two middle-aged women under the weight of overfull backpacks, one tall and thin, the other short and stout, approach and ask in halting Spanish where I got my coffee. For a moment, I think they're joking, but their faces are earnest and worried.

"Inside," I reply in English. "Just ask at the bar."

"Oh, thanks." Their relief is massive.

Judy and Susan are from Seattle and Denver. This is their first day on the Camino. Judy has wanted to walk the trail since seeing a movie about it a decade earlier, and her friend "likes to take walks" and so joined her. They're embarrassed to be only beginning and ask how long I've been walking. When I tell them, they look upon me with awe. I laugh.

The vast majority of walkers join the trail after Saint-Jean-Pied-de-Port.

In fact, most complete only the final one hundred kilometers—the last four or five days. I assure Judy and Susan that the trail is often much more enticing than the pavement-bound grind we have walked this morning. They nod, just happy to have coffee and a place to sit. I hoist my pack as they unlace their heavy boots.

A block down the road, just before the trail finally leaves pavement, I encounter Irish, whom I haven't seen in a week, and James, sitting at a table outside a small bar. James is manic and insists I join them.

"You must taste this orange juice. It's extraordinary."

I assure him I've just eaten. He won't hear it. I go inside and order an orange juice. The brooding girl behind the counter asks, "Are you with those two?"

"Is everything OK?" I ask. "*Está bien?*"

She doesn't answer me but looks unhappy.

Once outside again, James informs me that he and Irish have been up all night. It's only then that I realize they are both very drunk and high. Irish sits frozen and ramrod straight, glaring directly ahead, as if confronting an enemy only he can see. I'm not certain he's noticed me at all. James is unrestrained; he has had some major insights and wants to share them with me. I guzzle my juice and extract myself quickly. James tugs on my arm as I rise.

Once I cross the road and am finally on dirt again, I regret being rude to my friend but just as quickly realize he is so out of reality that it doesn't matter. I walk through vineyards. The grapes are heavy on the vine, deep purple and sweet. I eat handfuls at will. Spitting the tiny pits, I'm reminded of how long we have walked and how far we've traveled since Sam and I bit into the sour green pellets from the vines of La Rioja, outside Logroño. The ennui I felt this morning has been replaced in equal measure by contentment. After an hour, I enter the town of Cacabelos. It's a long road in, but opposite the tenth-century Church of Santa María, I drop my load beside a table outside an amiable bar, order a bocadillo de jamón, and kick off my shoes.

In short order, Ryan and Kylie come up the road. Kylie has been on the periphery of the group for a week and lately moves in lockstep with Ryan, who easily attracts women but, like a sparrow, seems to flit away as he feels closed in upon.

Irish then comes storming down the center of the road, his eyes blazing. "Your son is coming!" he shouts at me. "Your son is coming!" he shouts again, louder. And he's gone.

Chris arrives with the usual toothy grin on his face. Once he settles, he asks, "Did you see James?"

"I did," I say.

Chris produces a picture of our friend curled up asleep on the sidewalk beneath the table where I left him, his hat still on.

"He was very much awake when I left him," I say. Then, pointing at Chris's phone, I suggest, "You should delete that."

Ryan and Chris fill me in. Apparently, after leaving us at the sushi restaurant, James went directly to the albergue and was safely tucked in. Moments before the door was locked for the night, Irish arrived with some cocaine and acid. James got out of bed.

"Where is Irish finding acid around here?" I ask.

The boys shrug at my naivete just as Judy and Susan shuffle up. I invite them to join us, and their packs hit the ground before I've finished my sentence. I introduce them around.

"There, now you have nearly all the friends it's taken me four hundred miles to make."

Sam marches up the street to shouted greetings all around. He beams as he lowers his pack and pulls out tobacco to roll a cigarette.

"Coke, Sammy?" I ask.

"I'd love one, Dad. Thanks." He is all confidence and expansiveness.

At that moment, a cab comes down the town's single street. As it passes, the brake lights flare. Roger pokes his head out the window. "Hey, aren't you guys going to Villafranca?"

"We are," Chris says.

"Pull up a seat," Ryan says. "You must be starving after that long ride."

Everyone laughs, but Roger doesn't seem to notice. He takes a seat.

Sam leans close to me. "Dad, did you see Irish?"

"Yeah." I frown.

Sam shakes his head, "Man, if there's anyone who's killed someone, it's him."

"It's like Eden here"

115 miles to Santiago

"Get over onto the fucking road," I hiss as they pass.

"But this is the Camino," the biker shouts.

"You've got the whole road," I call back. But they're gone. "God, I fucking hate literal people," I say to Sam.

"And bikers," Sam adds.

We're climbing out of Villafranca. The trail, if you can use such a word, is a narrow strip of asphalt on the side of a highway, wedged between two crash barriers. While this is intended to provide protection from traffic, it imperils the walker to the stupidity of the bikers. A group of four whistling and shouting cyclists has just pinned us up against the guardrail so they could get by. To make matters worse, the wide road where they should be traveling is entirely empty—it's seldom used now because the new A-6 highway attracts the bulk of traffic.

I was already in a foul mood. I woke up at 4:15 and couldn't get back to sleep. We weren't able to find anything to eat before we left. A cloud of gnats has been swarming in my face for twenty minutes as the grade has steepened into a long hill. Sam is into a full nasal Bob Dylan impersonation.

"Sometimes the Camino sucks," I say.

"I could do another month of the Camino, Dad," Sam says. "I feel like I'm just getting into the groove."

We pass under the new highway; cars hum above us. The road we're on winds and climbs. Sam's buoyant mood eventually pulls me out of my

191

sour one. We talk Gen Z dynamics, which takes us on to the spectrum of sexuality, then without noticing quite how, to LSD—topics unlikely to be discussed at home when I see Sam for a few minutes at a time as he races out or I come in late from work.

In the village of Pereje, the obligatory adorable stray kitten scampers past and hurries under a rotted slat in the door of an abandoned building. In the village of Trabadelo, we run into Roger. He has walked a few miles today and is deciding from which village to order his taxi. "This one or the next?" he asks us. "It's almost four klicks away."

"Tough call, Roger," I say.

"You're hard on old Roger," Sam tells me once we've seen our friend into a cab and are on our way again.

"You're right, Sam," I confess. "I'm just not sure exactly what the hell he's doing."

"Walk your own Camino, bro." Sam uses my line against me.

In the village of Herrerías, we stop for lunch at the last bar in town, which is always a mistake. If it turns out to be a dump or the welcome is wanting, there's nothing to be done. Backtracking is never an option. We're presented with two fatty bocadillos on stale bread and surly service. Neither of us are satiated. The next few hours of walking are among the toughest of the Camino, to the mountaintop settlement of O Cebreiro.

Sam gets up to throw most of his sandwich away, and I ask him to toss mine as well.

"Do it yourself," he snaps.

"What?" I'm taken aback by the venom in his remark.

Apparently, Sam had said something to me that I hadn't heard. Consequently, I didn't answer him. Perhaps because we're getting tired and are still hungry and have a steep walk ahead, he took greater offense at this than he might normally. So when I asked for his aid after what he perceived was my blowing him off, he snapped at me. I'm not aware of any of this in the moment, and our fight quickly escalates. I need to remind him, and myself, to keep our voices down, as there are others in the establishment.

We stomp down the street in silence, passing a barn in which mules can be rented for the steep ascent up the mountain. (I give a quick glance inside. James had told me that his wife, prior to their meeting, had an affair with the mule-keeper, and James resents the man. I understand the emotion, but see only a few burros nibbling hay.) When we get to what is the clear base of the climb, the trail diverts onto a dirt track and up it goes.

Sam charges ahead, and I'm relieved.

The trail turns to stone and then becomes a golden dirt and climbs through a forest of mature Spanish chestnut trees. The way sinks into a trench so that a head-high wall of earth, rock, and exposed roots flank the walker. Coupled with the canopy of the overhanging trees, the sensation is of being swaddled, walking through a protected canal toward something even greater. The mountaintop village of O Cebreiro was the most memorable stop on my first Camino. Images of small stone buildings with thatched roofs and expansive views, a fine meal, and a personal Camino "miracle" have remained strong in my mind for a quarter century.

I plug in my earbuds and turn up the Gothic, adolescent melodrama of *Bat Out of Hell*, Meat Loaf's record from the mid 1970s. "Paradise by the Dashboard Light," wafting out of the basement stereo during a springtime party is indelibly intertwined with my first proper make-out session on the front lawn of a friend's house when I was in tenth grade— to this day, one of the most erotic experiences of my life. That I was too self-conscious to speak to the gentle girl come Monday morning takes nothing away from the love I've always felt toward her for what transpired between us for those ten minutes.

I've at times felt the grind, the wear and tear of this long walk upon my fifty-eight-year-old body, but pressing up the steepest incline of the Camino, endorphins kicking in, I have more power than I need. I'm almost running up the mountain. I pass a young couple collapsed on the side of the trail, guzzling water, looking bewildered. I don't pause but pump my fist in a gesture of solidarity and keep climbing.

I carry an indelible image from my first Camino of two butterflies leading me down the mountain the day out of O Cebreiro. Now, two brown and yellow butterflies flutter in front of my face and lead me up. I feel as if I'm being welcomed home. I pass another pilgrim doubled over on the side of the trail. "*Fuerza*"—"strength," I urge him, and climb on.

I barely notice the hamlet of La Faba and don't break stride in tiny Laguna de Castilla. I cross into the province of Galicia, the vista opens as the trail keeps climbing through scrubland. For more than an hour, the path is steeper than I recall at any point, steeper than the Pyrenees. My legs drive. I am pouring sweat. A small and well-tended patch of kale thrives beside the path. A large radio tower looms on a nearby summit. A stone wall begins to skirt the Camino. I'm under trees again, and then suddenly, there is Sam sitting on the stone wall at the crest of the mountain on the outskirts of O Cebreiro. He looks trepidatious as I approach—little wonder, given the mood in which we parted. I let out a war whoop, raise my arms over my head in victory, and wrap my son in a bear hug.

"Amazing walk, huh, Sammy?" I shout.

"Whoa, Dad, take it easy."

In the year 1300, Juan Santín walked through a blizzard to attend Mass at the mountaintop church of Santa María la Real. On arrival, the haughty local priest mocked the peasant, scoffing at the lengths the man would go to for some free bread and wine. In that instant, the Eucharist became body and blood—even the nearby statue of the Virgin Mary tilted her head to witness the act—and Pope Innocent VIII declared the event a miracle. O Cebreiro has been famous ever since. Queen Isabella passed this way while walking her Camino just a few years before sending Columbus off to find a new world, donating a reliquary to the church. Even the Holy Grail is said to have been housed here for a time.

My own miracle at O Cebreiro was less celebrated but nearly as wondrous. The sky had opened just as I arrived late in the afternoon twenty-six years earlier. In torrential rain, I went to the albergue and found it overfull to bursting. The one small pension in the village of twenty-six souls contained four rooms, and all were spoken for. The next village was a two-hour walk. Night fell. Uncertain what I would do, I sat down with other pilgrims for a communal dinner. A fire burned in the corner, warming the chilly night. Lightning flashed outside the small windows of the stone structure, thunder crashed as rain fell. Accepting that I would spend the night outside under the portico of the tiny church, I enjoyed a raucous dinner of fellowship among pilgrims relieved after the difficult climb. As dinner ended, the proprietress of the pension approached me and whispered in my ear that someone had not shown up to claim one of the four rooms. Would I like a bed for the night?

No transfiguration, but not bad.

This time I had called ahead. The village has become more popular since my last visit, and a few more of the old buildings have been converted to small inns. Even so, all were booked. Each day for the past two weeks I checked, but with no luck. This morning when I called again, a room had finally cleared. A night under the portico has been skirted again.

The village is—for once—exactly as I remember it. Except that in the ensuing years, the bus-tour trade has discovered this mountaintop haven. Hungry trinket-hunters swoop into the three souvenir shops (new since last trip) for a scallop shell or a yellow-arrow pin, perhaps light a candle in the rack outside the church, snap a photo of the vista, stare at the smelly pilgrims as if we're in a free-range zoo, then climb back onto the bus. The locals understand that these tourists spend more and require less than the pilgrims who have been the life blood of this village for centuries, so that we now often receive disinterested service. O Cebreiro is a victim of its own success. But as with many overloved locales, once the last bus leaves, tranquility descends again, and the place returns to its natural idyllic state—even more welcoming for having survived the daily onslaught.

Night is slow to fall in a cloudless sky, the last light lingering late. I wander, then sit on a stone wall looking out over the valley to the south and west, pink light fading. Then, in the one minute it takes to walk back across the village, I gaze over the valley to the north and east, where night has already fallen. I stand looking up to the window of the room where I stayed last time. I am trying to further imprint this place on my psyche. Sam chats late into the evening outside a bar with The White People and a young man from Korea, whom we haven't met before.

Before sunrise, I'm back sitting in the same spot on the same stone wall. The wind is ripping over the mountaintop. The moon is still high and approaching full, casting shadows on the ground. Clouds are low in the valley below. The sky goes purple, then gently pink, asking permission for the new day. Dawn chases the wind away. I miss my wife.

Sam and I dawdle over breakfast, in no rush to leave. When Sam spills his coffee, neither of us is startled or even surprised and we wipe it up without acknowledgment and keep chatting. The Boys, Ryan and Chris, arrive. They stayed down in the village below last night and set out early. We order another coffee, glad for the excuse to loiter.

"I saw a taxi waiting out there," Chris says, "Is Roger here?"

When we finally push back our chairs, step outside, and hoist our packs, Sam looks around one last time—O Cebreiro still tranquil before the first bus arrives. Birds call. A mild breeze blows.

"It's like Eden here, Dad."

"More harm than good"

Although the greater world might reasonably argue that this walk has no real purpose, that it achieves no practical goals, and so is of no merit or consequence, there's a growing awareness among us, without being able to quite name it yet, that what we are doing is somehow of import and has meaning. Each day's walk creates more internal space, even as the exact alchemy of it eludes us. We still have nearly a hundred miles to Santiago, but there's a feeling of assurance on the trail today. And the topic of confidence is bandied about.

"In something like the Camino, it is what it is," I say. "The difficulty or challenge is apparent, and overcoming it produces a certain internal result in proportion to your sense of personal achievement. You can feel it, right? It feels solid, it's real, you own it. And it feels good."

"Undoubtedly," Sam says.

"It's when things are not so easily quantified that there can be problems."

"What do you mean?" Sam asks.

"Often, there's an overassertion that appears as confidence but is really just deep insecurity turned on its head. That's when things get dangerous."

"You're not talking about Matthew McConaughey again, are you?"

I laugh. "No, I think he actually does believe. But mental health is a different topic."

It's Sam's turn to laugh. "Forget about McConaughey. But that kind of behavior you're talking about fools a lot of people."

"Oh, for sure. Including the person who's behaving with that bravado, or arrogance, or whatever you want to call it."

"And that's why confirmation bias exists."

"What exactly is confirmation bias?" I ask.

"Just what you're talking about. Basically, only hanging around with people who buy into your crap, or just reading shit you agree with."

"Exactly."

The trail skirts the edge of the mountain, revealing vast views to the north. It dips and then climbs steeply and briefly to Alto de San Roque, and a well-positioned café at the crest of the rise seems unprepared for its popularity. Outdoor tables are littered with dirty dishes, the few staff are hassled, my tortilla Española is undercooked. A chicken scampers underfoot.

I meet a middle-aged woman and her husband who have just joined the Camino for the last week of the walk. She works for a large tech company in Seattle.

"We have some big life decisions to make," Marcia tells me. "We thought this might help."

"Well, it'll get you away from your computer for a few days," I say. "That can't hurt."

She nods, unsure. "I hope so."

The trail plunges as Sam laments what he calls "those damn Camino trend-surfers"—pilgrims like Marcia and her husband. There are more and more fresh faces with new backpacks and pale limbs the farther west we migrate, and Sam is none too happy about it.

"Frauds." He dismisses the newcomers with a wave of his hand.

Then—I'm not sure exactly how—the topic turns to school. "School lowered what I perceived I'm capable of," Sam says. "It did me more harm than good." There is suddenly real emotion in his voice, real hurt. This is not fresh hurt, like the hurt he has been working through regarding The Ex, but a more saturated hurt. A hurt he has carried for years, for most of his life. It is the hurt born of lazy definition and judgment thrown heavily upon him like a wet overcoat. A hurt that blindsided him, then threatened to define him. His is the hurt of someone who was misunderstood and dismissed out of hand, before he had a chance to define his own experience. It is a hurt that, for a time, came closer to swallowing my son than I knew. It is a hurt with calcified edges.

Beginning in the first grade, when at a typical parent teacher/meeting in which Sam's mother and I expected to chat with his teacher for fifteen minutes about our son's block-stacking prowess, a half dozen people, including the head of the school, and several others I'd never seen, gathered to wave red flags over Sam's potential "learning challenges." And the next year, in a new school, during our first meeting, we were cautioned that our son would likely be "counseled out"—removed from school. And it went on, year after year. Tutoring. Emergency conferences. Various forms of testing were recommended and undertaken. Drugs were pushed and resisted. Then, early in high school, a classmate confessed to Sam that she was considering suicide and began sending him disturbing videos. When Sam, with my encouragement, reported this to school authorities, he was punished, the incident twisted and used as an excuse to expel him. My son had been branded, and his every action was seen through the lens of their settled judgment.

And I failed him. Confusion and fear took hold early and hung over my reactions. "So he doesn't sit perfectly still, so what!" I shouted more than once and was escorted from more than one office by people who cloaked themselves in a superior headshaking posture of concern. These people didn't know my son. Why would they not see him? What I didn't understand then was that the institutions, all institutions, protect themselves first, no matter the platitudes and slogans they boast.

Sam's mother, his stepmother, even his sister, did their best to be reasonable. I did not. We were under siege. The tide had to be held back.

Add to this the nightly anger I directed toward Sam over undone homework went far beyond reason and only compounded an already troubled situation. That my son didn't turn from me and walk away from our relationship is testament to his character.

For years, my family teased me that I was sure to break down into sobs at Sam's eventual high school graduation, but when the day arrived, I felt only relief it was over and shame that I had not better served my son. He was just another student who didn't fit the mold and had been thus discarded.

In the village of Fonfría, we come upon a small earth digger beside a garbage truck in the middle of the road. The arm of the digger raises its shovel up into the air, and then it dives toward the ground. The lifeless body of a calf is pinned between the teeth of the shovel and hoisted high, its limbs and torso hanging limp. The digger swivels its arm above the truck as the animal's hooves sway, its head swings. The shovel opens, and gravity pulls the animal out of sight into the back of the truck with an echoing thud. Discarded.

"If the Pacific Northwest and Colorado had a baby," Ryan says, waving his walking stick out over the rolling, dramatic landscape, "this would be it." The Boys and Kylie have caught up and are bopping down the trail with us. The path, continuing to fall and rise and fall, grows soft underfoot. The air is mild, an almost imperceptible breeze blows. Expansive views present themselves in the gaps of dense foliage. Cows lumber in fields, their bells clanging. It's a fine day for walking.

Outside the village of Triacastela, several massive, old and knotted chestnut trees keep watch. The town is stretched out along a single narrow road. Our lodging is in a stone building that's been imaginatively restored. Twenty-five years ago, there was no such care given to once-dilapidated structures. This entire village is a testament to the increased popularity of the Camino.

Sam and Chris decide to go for a jog back up the trail we just descended.

"Fifteen miles was enough for me, but you go for it, dude," I tell Sam when he asks if I think him nuts for doing so. "I'll be here keeping vigil."

I'm teasing, of course, but I'm also resending what I hope is a larger message. The most important message I could send to my adult child. I'm here. For you—when you need, or want, and even when you don't. I'm here.

When I first left home and moved to New York and felt so adrift, so on my own in the big city, my father would often pay me a visit unannounced. My buzzer would simply sound at any hour. "Hey, pal!" would come my father's habitual greeting over the scratchy intercom, and up he'd come, or I'd be instructed to meet him down on the stoop. We never discussed anything of consequence, and such encounters were always brief. You would be hard-pressed to say these meetings passed for intimacy, and I hated these surprise visits—"raids" I called them. But they had an effect, intended or otherwise, of letting me know that I was not alone, that someone was out there, if not keeping watch or taking care, at least someone was aware of my existence at a time when I was all but invisible.

I walk the town, then settle outside a rustic restaurant at a picnic table under a giant hydrangea in gaudy bloom. Its violet pom-poms hang heavy. Roger spots me and detours over. He sits, informing me that his girlfriend is joining him tomorrow and that together they will be walking the last several days to Santiago.

"Walking?"

"I've been resting the knee. We're going to take a few extra days. I can make it." The tone in his voice is asking for reassurance. I oblige.

"You'll make it." While Sam is of course right when he tells me to 'walk my own Camino' in reference to Roger, I still can't help but wonder what Roger tells himself. Does he believe he has walked this far across Spain? I don't have the heart to ask.

Morgan and Alex stroll up, hand limply in hand. The small man from Sri Lanka still wears the smirk of a geek who can't believe his luck in scoring this pretty blond, while Morgan seems, as she always does, a bit remote and bemused at herself. I've had an affection for her since the evening in Mazarife when she wondered openly at her actions in breaking off with her boyfriend who had come from America to propose.

"How've you two kids been getting on?" I ask. "I haven't seen you in a few days."

"We've been sleeping in and walking late," Alex confides, his voice full of innuendo. It seems like he might even wink at me. He talks of their probable future together, commuting between London and Alabama. Morgan stares off, a wan smile on her face.

Theresa, the Belgian woman I met back in Burgos, the one who was so interested in me discussing what lessons I had learned along the Camino, appears and takes a seat. She is as earnest and seeking as ever.

Ryan and Kylie enter, both happy and bright.

Suddenly, Irish whirls around the hydrangea, its pom-poms shaking in his wake.

"Kiren!" the table lets out a shout. No one has seen him in days. He nods, ducking his head, and takes a seat. His face is pulled tight, his eyes red-rimmed.

"Have some food, Kiren," I suggest.

"No, I couldn't eat," he says, avoiding all eye contact. "I'll just have a beer."

Ryan gets the waiter's attention.

Sam and Chris arrive.

"How was the run?" I ask.

"Hard," Sam says, looking slightly disoriented, even after a shower. When he tells the waiter he wants the beef tongue for dinner, I wonder if he knows what he's just ordered.

It recalls a moment from my first Camino. An older woman in a small village had hung a sign outside her door, offering pilgrims a home-cooked meal for a cheap price. The only restaurant in town had burst a pipe and was closed. So along with several others, I sat around her dining room table, clear plastic covering the chairs to keep our pilgrim filth from soiling her furniture. A large hunk of beef was placed on the table before us. To my surprise, I found it tender and flavorful, but slightly different in texture than anything I had eaten before. As I took a second helping, the woman came out of the kitchen. I asked what cut of beef this was. She said a word I didn't understand, and seeing my confusion, she touched the tip of her finger to her tongue. I gagged on the piece in my mouth and was unable to eat any more. I've never been able to eat beef tongue.

Roger proposes we go around the table and all offer up our single best Camino "tip." I'm immediately embarrassed and want to leave. Everyone else settles in and gives the matter serious consideration. The Belgian seeker is excited by the topic and volunteers several suggestions.

Tips that combine both literal advice and symbolic significance seem to be those most praised. "Walk, don't reach" is a popular catchphrase, the exact meaning of which eludes me. I wonder what it is about myself that is made so uncomfortable by such forced camaraderie. When it comes around the table to me, I mutter something about how my tip would be to not give advice.

"Oh, come on, Dad," Sam prods.

"Yeah, come on, Dad," Ryan teases, and the others join in.

For a minute, I'm the butt of good-natured ribbing, until Irish falls off his bench without warning. We help him up and get him settled back.

He is unconcerned by the fall. Ryan leaves an arm around Kiren's shoulder and conversation continues.

"How's the tongue?" I ask Sam.

"It's not bad, actually. Kind of got a fuzzy coat, but good."

Chris and Sam solidify their plans to go to Finisterre together.

"We're gonna do it in two days, though," Sam says.

"That's a long way in two days," Kylie warns him.

"Maybe for some," Sam boasts. The table laughs. Then someone asks if I'll be going along.

"No," I explain, "Santiago is my goal."

"Yeah, my dad is walking across *most* of Spain," Sam says, a glint in his eye. "I'm walking across *all* of Spain."

"You chose it"

84 miles to Santiago

"What are you doing?" I croak.

"Did I wake you?"

"It's the middle of the fucking night, of course you woke me." Sam is surprised that I find this problematic.

"Oh, sorry. I'm just washing my clothes," he whispers soothingly. "Go back to sleep."

One of the most important lessons I've learned while walking across Spain with my son is to get into the bathroom and take a shower before he does. Sam manages to soak every inch of every bathroom and use every towel, no matter the size or configuration of the room or the amount of linen on offer. I've gotten used to it. I have made adjustments and accommodations, the way only a parent does for those they love and favor. But this idea of doing laundry in the sink at midnight is new. I do my best to roll over.

The next morning, we set out late. Even though I lost an hour or two of sleep, I woke, as usual, in the predawn. Sam did not. But as we had only a short twelve miles to walk today, I didn't press the matter.

The road rises up and out of town. At the crest of a hill in the middle distance, two windmills sit idle; the blades of a third can be seen just beyond the rise, turning with the sluggish determination of the righteous.

Sam is holding forth on the benefits of intermittent fasting.

"I always thought you were supposed to eat as soon after waking up as possible," I say, "so that you're a 'food burner' and not a 'food storer.'"

"Who told you that?"

"Um..."

"No." Sam dismisses my belief of twenty years with a swipe of his hand.

Ahead, apple trees line the trail. Already, clusters of bruised fruit sit on the ground beneath the branches, rotting. The stench of decay mixed with their sweet smell brings me instantly back to the annual apple-picking outing I force upon my family. "Dad, I love you," my daughter, Willow, said last fall, "but do we have to do this again next year?"

"What's the matter with you?" I demanded. "This is as good as it gets."

My wife made a cringing face, "Nnnnn..."

My youngest, Rowan, cut to the chase. "Can I wait in the car?"

An unseen dog barks out warning when we pass through a deserted village. Entering a lush forest, the grade stiffens. Moss covers the stone walls flanking the path. A small van is parked on the trail, the words "Conservacion del Camino de Santiago" painted on its side. In front of it, a man in a white jumpsuit and reflective yellow vest is bending to lift a twig from the path. The Camino has become big business, life-sustaining business, for the towns along its course, and the intent is to keep it that way. This is particularly evident here in Galicia, where so many join the trail for the final push to the Cathedral in Compostela. Way markers, once encountered only intermittently during the day and approached with excitement, are now placed several to a kilometer and become meaningless in their frequency, placed perhaps to reassure those new to the trail.

"Goddamn newbies," Sam laments.

"Not everybody has the time, Sammy. It's a long walk."

"Or they're just lazy and want the credit without the investment."

At Alto de Riocabo, the high point in elevation for the day's walk, the valleys below are veined with clouds. We travel a worn tarmac road and come upon two arrows painted on the pavement, one pointing down the road we're on and the other, more faded, directing off down a more narrow, ungraded lane. I veer off to follow this seemingly less trodden way.

"Where are you going?" Sam asks.

"It's probably just an alternate. Let's go this way, get away from the main road."

Sam shakes his head and follows. The old lane climbs over a rise, then turns to dirt. No further markers or arrows are in evidence.

"This is wrong, Dad."

"Let's just go a little farther," I say. "I bet it comes around to the right and meets up after that bend."

The track turns left. Then it dips and rises and swings into a long arc as Sam announces that he is no longer going to do chest exercises. "I just look at a weight and my chest gets bigger." He conveys this with the seriousness of a man reconsidering brain surgery.

As a boy, Sam was slight—as was I—and early in puberty found his way to weight lifting. The gym increased his confidence while worrying his parents with fears of altered growth plates and nightmares of steroid abuse. Yet the result of Sam's passion utterly transformed his self-image from one of fragility and insecurity to physical assurance.

We pass fields of corn and pastures with idle cows. The absence of yellow arrows or any of the recently ubiquitous stanchions is glaringly evident. We pass a man driving a tractor pulling a cart in a field, just off the track. He looks over and, upon seeing us, he laughs. Of all the farmers we have passed over these hundreds of miles, none has reacted to us, save for an occasional nod of the head or the rare lifting of a finger from the steering wheel, in acknowledgment of our presence.

"That guy just laughed at us," Sam says.

"It did look like that, didn't it?"

"No, it didn't look like it. He did."

And then we're walking in fog. Thick fog.

"Think we should go back?" I ask.

"You chose it."

"You can't just keep going if you know you're wrong," I say.

"It was your idea to go this way," Sam snaps.

"Yes, I am aware of that. I'm just saying that you have to correct course when you misjudge."

I'm now attaching larger meaning to this debate. I'm suddenly anxious that my son will feel inclined to follow a mistake to tragic ends simply because pride or laziness prevent a judicious recalculation. Despite the fact that I am the one who made this mistake, my anxiety spurs a need to instruct as I contemplate my son's apparently dubious judgment. For this reason, I feel the need to turn back, to show Sam that admitting mistakes and making adjustments is mature and prudent policy. Yet, in a corner of my mind, I also hear my wife's voice, reminding me that I have a tendency to give up just a moment too soon—to quit "five minutes before the miracle." These competing narratives are doing battle, when I notice that Sam has pulled out his phone.

"We can keep going this way," he says, staring down at the screen. "It'll be longer than if we had stayed on the road but shorter than if we go back." He offers up the phone to me, and I see his little green Snapchat man chugging along a dirt track on the map, far off the Camino. With a series of judicious and carefully attended turns, we can regain the main road in a mile or so.

"Oh, piece of cake," I say. "And look at all this nice countryside we got to see."

"Is that supposed to be disarming sarcasm?" Sam looks at his phone. "Turn left here."

As if on cue, once we regain the main road the sun burns through, and our foggy detour is relegated to that of a misty unreality. We come upon a stone farmhouse that's been converted to include a small café in its front room, complete with outdoor tables on the small stone porch. The place is nearly full with older walkers new to the trail. We find the last empty table outside at Casa do Franco. Middle-aged Alberto and his wife, Angeles, him dark, her fair, are scrambling to serve the crowd, all the while with bright smiles and friendly patter. Beneficiaries of geographic good fortune with their home on a slip road beside the Camino, they've concluded that it's more profitable to press coffee than shovel the manure.

Sam rolls a cigarette. "I'm getting better at these." He holds the burning smoke aloft.

"I'm not sure that's such a good thing," I say.

We carry on over open rolling hills abutting farming land. We pass through the village of Pintin, where the stench of animal excrement is strong. Rolled bales of hay are stacked in crumbling enclosures.

"There's a gym in Sarria," Sam says. "I'm going to grind fifteen sets of chest."

"I thought you weren't doing chest," I say.

"Hey, fuck you," Sam barks, his tone suddenly harsh. "You don't lift."

"Don't talk to me like that," I warn him. "You just said you didn't want to work chest anymore."

Sam bolts up the trail.

Our children are adept at reading subtext even when we're not astute enough to recognize it ourselves. My remark, while appearing to be a simple response to his earlier statement, was, at least in part, motivated by something else, my concern that he might get too muscle-bound for his height and make himself appear stocky. I was in essence calling him short.

I watch my son storm off. I pass through another largely deserted village. The smell of manure is almost overpowering, rose plants grow wild, most of the roofs are crumbling. I grow more and more upset with Sam, clinging to the words he used while pushing away any accountability for the unspoken messaging for which I was responsible. I blow past him waiting on the edge of Sarria and march up the hill to the center of town.

"You can't speak to me like that. I obviously upset you, but I would never say that to you, and it's not OK to say it to me."

"You're right. I'm sorry."

With a population of nearly fifteen thousand, Sarria has more on its mind than just the Camino. The trail skirts only one corner of the bustling town, with most pilgrim services clustered along a single road. Sam drops his pack and heads to the gym. Our accommodation is a reclaimed stable recently and elegantly renovated by an equally elegant man named Javier, who came here from Barcelona. "I don't know why," he confesses. "I always wanted to do something like this." He waves his hand out over his rustic-chic property. "If it doesn't work, I just lose my money and I will go back." His attitude is both stoic and cavalier. "But I love it."

When Sam returns, he suggests a typically downtrodden pilgrim restaurant he saw just up the road. I insist on a good meal at a steakhouse Javier has recommended on the other side of town. A half hour walk, condescending service, and an excessive bill later, we trudge back toward our converted stable. We pass the pilgrim restaurant Sam suggested earlier, and a wave of laughter rolls out onto the street to mock me.

"I'm sorry, Sam. You were right."

"About what?"

"All of it."

He shrugs. "Obvs."

"The zombie apocalypse"

72 miles to Santiago

Sarria occupies a unique position along the Camino. Situated just over a hundred kilometers from Santiago, it is the last point along the trail from which a walker may begin and still receive a Compostela, the official document certifying that the bearer has traversed the Camino de Santiago and is entitled to the indulgences such an effort bestows—read: bragging rights.

Consequently, the trail now feels packed. "This really is the zombie apocalypse!" Sam moans as we grind up Calle Mayor past the Praza da Constitución, flanked by cafés and pilgrim hostels. Nervous chatter fills the air as scores of new walkers cinch stiff backpacks and stretch untested limbs while sipping coffee. I spot Marcia, the woman who works for the large tech company with the "big decisions to make" who began a few days earlier. She and her husband, Bob, wear somewhat bewildered smiles. "A bit sore, but all good," she assures me, and I chase Sam, who has not slowed, up the hill.

The air this morning is close, an early fog hangs. Our ascent is over soft umber dirt through mature oak and knotted chestnuts, between ivy- and moss-covered stone walls. Dew hangs from ferns blanketed in ornate spiderwebs. Horses droop their heads over fences hoping for a snack, or at least a pet. Apple trees hang heavy with swollen fruit. An older couple is visible through a field, tending a fecund garden. We cross a running stream over granite stepping-stones. The fog is burned off and the sun slashes through the foliage, dappling our way. The walking is sublime.

Even a crowing rooster can't spoil Sam's appreciation of the terrain. "This trail is like the Greatest Hits of the Camino," he says. As with the verdant Irish countryside to which it is so similar, Galicia on a mild and sunny day is difficult to top.

But then there are those people. All those new people. After a few hours, we come upon the first café of the day. It is overflowing. "If you're any younger than sixty-five and older than seven, you should be ashamed of yourselves," Sam declares to all assembled. Some heads turn. Others look down.

"Let's find the next one," I say, touching Sam's arm.

"My contempt for these new people knows no bounds," he assures me as we turn to go. "Charlatans!" he calls out over his shoulder.

"You might want to practice a little Camino compassion," I suggest.

"Look, I've had other things to work through on this walk. I'll get to the self-actualization next time."

"I'm not sure that's the word you're looking for."

"I know, but you know what I mean," he says.

I do. Once the dominant topic of discussion for days and weeks on end, we have rarely mentioned The Ex of late. Sam appears to be moving on. Further enlightenment can wait.

In the village of Barbadelo, a proud-looking man stands before a stone building offering painted scallop shells, a few Camino T-shirts, and walking sticks protruding from an umbrella stand. He gives us a grave nod as we pass. Apparently, this kind of capitalism has been going on here for some time. Back in the twelfth century, French scholar Aymeric Picaud wrote what was, in essence, the first guidebook to the Camino de Santiago, known as the *Codex Calixtinus*. It was chock-a-block with handy information on Saint James the Great, reports of miracles, sermons, and even a few songs, as well as a description of the route to Santiago. It dismissed this tiny hamlet as being all but destroyed by crass commercialism. I'm not sure what was on offer back in the day, but you'd be hard-pressed to begrudge this simple operation—although the perfume of manure has probably remained pretty constant over the centuries.

Beyond the town of Portomarín, over a rickety metal footbridge above the Río Miño, we head into a forested climb. The majority of people beginning in Sarria stop for the day in Portomarín, taking five days to walk to Santiago. Those of us who have been on the trail longer tend to keep walking and make it in four. This has the beneficial effect of putting us on a different timing to most of the newer walkers, and the trail once again feels thinly populated.

Beyond a pine forest blanketed in dense aroma, the land opens out. The trail is conspicuously empty of people; the afternoon sky grows hazy. We pass a noxious-smelling fertilizer plant, and the path begins to parallel the main road. Over such uninspired terrain, we put our heads down and grind out the miles. Sam plugs in his earbuds and marches ahead, singing. Soon he begins, as if drawn, to veer out into the road. I scream after him until he turns. From a great distance, I can see the irritation on his face. I wave him out of the road. He waves back, understanding now, even appreciative (?), and he moves over, as if this is the first time the idea that the road might be a thing of danger has been mentioned.

The land here feels drained of life. Cars roar past. I've had enough. Had we been at the start of the day—as this part of the trail will be for those who stop in Portomarín—this land would simply be an unmemorable few hours, but for us—for me—tired, hot, and hungry, it feels desolate and almost wrong, as if we have somehow veered far from the vibrant pulse of the Camino. We pass through a desolate village.

Then I see a sign for a guesthouse I had read good things about. In an instant, I decide we should change plans and stay here. I walk up the path to the house. The door is locked, but as this is often the case with family-run inns, I press my nose against the window and peer inside. I can see the lower half of a figure lying on the couch. I walk around to the side door. It's open. The figure on the couch is an elderly man, and he looks up at me with confusion as I cross the room. "*Buenos tardes,*" I say. An older woman, apparently the man's wife, enters. She spots me approaching her prone and frail husband with a large stick and begins to shout, loud and frightened. I spin at the sound. She is waving her arms. I back away.

In a few minutes, the misunderstanding is cleared up. They have been closed for the entire season, the woman tells me. Her husband is ill—that explains why no one ever answered the phone after my repeated calls. I apologize and shuffle off.

The encounter adds to the feeling that we have somehow stepped into some strange parallel universe. We wanted to be free from all those new walkers, and now we are. There is no one anywhere.

In time, we come upon the settlement of Castromayor. It also has no services, no restaurants, no shops. Our accommodation is a self-check-in situation. There is no one here either.

"Where the fuck are we, Dad?"

"I have no idea, Sam. It's weird, right?"

Sam consults his phone. "I got no signal."

According to the *Codex Calixtinus,* this area was forsaken even in the twelfth century—the nearby woods filled with prostitutes. Those caught indulging, according to the manual, would have their noses cut off.

Sam stares out the window, into the trees. "I'm going to walk back to the albergue. Maybe we can get some food there." We passed a small, paint-peeling pilgrim hostel a mile back.

"Good idea. I'll meet you after I do my laundry."

I trudge back though overgrown fields along a narrow footpath to the albergue, and in a glance the Camino makes sense again. Sam is sitting around a table playing cards with The Boys, Chris and Ryan, as well as

Kylie and a few Italians we know. They're all laughing, drinking beers or water. Sam and the Italians are smoking.

In our household Sam is notoriously unwilling to play games of any kind. "Come on, Sam," Willow always says. "Participate. It doesn't matter if you're no good."

"Want to play?" Chris asks me now.

"No." I shake my head. "I'm good." Until one becomes a parent, the notion of taking great pleasure in the idea of simply watching one's offspring is incomprehensible. Yet seeing my son now, making mistakes, discarding wrong cards, laughing at himself and being willing to not know, enjoying being taught—it's enough to tell me that our time in Spain has been well spent.

We join the dozen staying at the hostel around a large outdoor table for a typical pilgrim meal, short on delicacy and rich with camaraderie. The husband-and-wife team running the hostel and serving us are both harried and patient. Ice cream bars are handed out for dessert and are received with much fanfare.

Ryan gets up to retrieve his clothes from the line. Small clusters form and re-form. Laughter erupts and subsides. Sam rolls a cigarette for an attractive Italian woman. Then lights it for her. The evening grows quiet. Drifting back to our accommodations, wispy cirrus clouds are dyed crimson in a lingering sky.

"That was a real Camino evening," I say.

"That was a real good evening," Sam corrects me.

"Sheeeeeeech!"

53 miles to Santiago

I'm met with a permeating coolness when I walk out the door. The season has begun to change. Gone are the dry hot mornings foreshadowing blistering afternoons that dominated so much of our Camino. The sun is late, yet to come over the horizon. The sky is pushing away a hazy purple gray. The door closes behind me as a blackbird, a large one, lands on the wire before me, a few feet above my head. I stare at it. The bird doesn't move. Another, identical looking, lands beside it. The first doesn't give any outward indication of noticing the arrival of the second. But the two are clearly together. I stand watching the pair for another minute.

I'm watching, but really I'm waiting. Waiting in vain, I know. Sam was still in bed when I walked out.

"I'll catch up quick. I'm just taking my time, but I'm up," he said as I walked out.

It seems silly now, so much of the prodding and pulling, the shouting and threatening to get my son out of bed that characterized the mornings of our early walk. I'm reminded of advice I received soon after Sam was born. A friend's father, a man from a small Southern town, with a small town's Southern accent to match, saw the fear in my eyes and took my arm. "Andy," he purred, "you just love 'em, and keep 'em dry. The rest works out."

The first bird flies off, followed by the second. Their wings are athletic, urgent in their initial thrust from the wire. Then quickly they settle into ease and are gone, over the barn. Singular. Together.

The trail climbs steeply and briefly over open country. Clouds fill the valley to the north under pastel sky. Heather grows beside the dirt path. My footfalls are the only sound. When the sun breaks the horizon over my shoulder, my shadow before me is so long it has no form, and a soft breeze begins to push around the long and wispy, golden grass covering the hills. I snap my hundredth, my thousandth, photo of a Spanish sunrise. There's a brief detour off the trail to the site of an ancient ruin. The night before, I read about it and concluded it was worthy of a look. Today I have no interest in adding steps and keep to the path.

I hear a voice. I turn and Sam is cresting the hill, silhouetted by the rising sun—the outline of his form undeniable.

"I'm hungry," Sam says.

"Yeah, I know," I say.

There was no breakfast, no services; no one was ever present at our lodging. A bed was provided and no welcome. Perhaps that's where my feeling of emptiness came from this morning—the sense of being so transient, so temporary. Or maybe it's because I know we are close to the end of our walk, that this time out of time with my son is winding down. This bubble is about to burst.

My body is ready to finish. I'm tired. It's time, I know. And yet...

We walk past fields with sleeping cows, fields with rolled and drying hay, fields of ferns, and rows of neatly planted pines. A small working village smells of manure. Yellow arrows point west. When we pass a crowing rooster, Sam points threateningly at him. Few people are in evidence. We pass a cemetery. We pass an empty soccer field. More corn, rolling hills, distant windmills. At 10:00 a.m. it is suddenly hot.

Sam talks of The Ex for the first time in days. In the silence since his last mention of her, he has clearly been processing.

There is a clarifying distance in his perspective. "Onward," he concludes simply.

Then he talks of 4/20.

"What does 4/20 have to do with pot?" I ask.

"Dad, don't be that guy."

"I'm sorry, Sammy. Your fascination with marijuana, drugs, altered states, worries me."

"Well, that's your issue, Dad. Not mine."

"I know, Sammy."

We come upon a quiet café. I take a seat at a picnic table out front while Sam goes in and waits at the bar. For a long time. No wonder there are no other customers.

Then I hear it.

Over the past week or so, Sam has begun, at random times and with increasing frequency, to let out a holler/scream/exclamation— "Sheeeeeecch!"

What exactly this means, I have no idea, but I have come to interpret it as a kind of joyful howl— life force is rushing through him, with the overflow manifesting in this charming/obnoxious outburst. It began during one of his phone calls to his buddies back home, and my reaction to it has become a barometer for measuring my mood toward my son. Sometimes I laugh, other times I barely notice it, and occasionally I've snapped, "Please, shut up." I even tried it once at Sam's urging. The sound came out like an aborted sneeze.

"Never mind, Dad," Sam said patiently.

Now, from inside, I hear, "Sheeeeeecch!" come echoing out. I don't think he's calling for service; I don't think Sam is even aware that he's making the sound. At last, a man comes through the curtain of beads leading to a back room behind the bar.

Sam has fried eggs, then an ice cream cone, then tuna fish straight from the can. He finishes this breakfast of champions by spilling his coffee—twice.

Mopping up the table for the second time, I look at my son. "You haven't lost your touch, Sammy."

He shrugs an "I-mean-I-don't-know-what-can-I-say-it's-just-me-it's-not-like-I'm-trying-to-spill-stuff-all-the-time" shrug.

When we come upon the town of Palas de Rei, it is situated on a hilltop, and we're moving with pace down its steep and narrow lanes. This town is the major overnight stopover for those who joined the trail a few days ago. The cafés are already swarming.

"It's amazing how just a little change of timing and sync, and we don't see any of these people on the trail," I say.

"Damn newbies," Sam mutters.

Just clearing town, we see a lone pilgrim walking back along the trail toward us.

"What's this guy doing?" I ask.

The figure grows, and Sam shouts out, a smile in his voice. "Kiren!"—aka Irish.

He's marching toward us, walking the way he always does—head down, right shoulder pushed forward, torso inclined as if looking for dropped coins or ready for a brawl.

"I think Santiago is the other direction," I say.

"Ryan texted me." Kiren stops before us and shouts. "He's with some folks at some pilgrim place."

"There are a million pilgrims in that town," Sam says.

Kiren frowns, looking over my shoulder as if to see the swarm.

"He could drop you a pin with their location," Sam says.

"Yeah, sure. I can't do that shit," Irish brushes away the idea like a mosquito. "I left my pack in the woods back there."

"You left it in the woods?" Sam asks, trying to keep incredulity out of his voice—he may as well have said, "Are you a fucking idiot?"

"You don't think that's a good idea?" Kiren says. There's both challenge and genuine questioning in his voice.

"I'm sure it's fine," I say. "Who's gonna wander off into the woods and want a backpack?"

"You still have all your laundry hanging off it?" Sam asks.

"Yeah," Irish assures him.

"You're fine," Sam concludes.

With that, Kiren pushes past and up the hill. Sam and I look at each other, neither feeling the need to speak.

The trail now becomes idyllic. Deeply established walking paths bisect well-tended and soft-edged fields. The leaves of trees, their trunks swaddled in ivy, dapple light over golden, gently receptive earth. Up and down it goes over mild hills that succeed only in creating a constantly changing, cinematic experience of an intimate expanse. And then there's one particular field beside a particularly gracious bit of trail. It is much like the others, only more so. Its dozen cows stand still in the shade. The bordering fences are covered in thick ivy and lush moss. I stop. It's as if the colors here are just slightly brighter, more vibrant, the dappling just a bit more magical, the cows more handsome. The breeze feels slightly cooler. The air is sweet.

"Wow," I say, then look over at Sam.

"This one is an eleven." He nods.

And then we come upon our first eucalyptus grove. Planted en masse in Galicia as agriculture became less and less profitable, the fast-growing, invasive, distinctive-smelling eucalyptus became a profitable alternative. Useful for lumber and pulp, the peeling bark and almond-shaped leaves somehow became the talisman of my first Camino. For twenty-six years, it has been impossible for me to smell the medicinal-citrus-mint-honey aroma and not think of my final joyful days along my first trek. The unconscious mind is a funny thing—we are often not the one to decide what is meaningful to us.

"Wait till we get to the eucalyptus forests," I've said to Sam more than once over the past month. And at the first strand of mature, straight-trunked eucalyptus, Sam walks off the trail, then deep down a row of trees, touching the shredding, peeling bark, and breathing deep. After a few minutes he returns to the trail.

"That's cool." He nods, protruding his lower lip. I'm glad he sees what I see in them. Or is he seeing things that way because we are feeling close and, in an act of unconscious generosity, has allowed them to take on meaning for him simply because they have meaning for me. I suppose that's as good a definition of love as any. I breathe the forest perfume.

After such soothing nature, the working town of Melide feels larger and more chaotic than its seventy-five hundred inhabitants. I suggest Sam text The Boys and see if they want to have dinner.

The local specialty here is boiled octopus served with olive oil and paprika, Pulpo a la Gallega. As a small child, Sam fell in love with octopus and has gone out of his way to get it whenever he can. To my unsophisticated palate, it's always tasted like rubber.

"Let's you and me go eat pizza," Sam says.

"I'll never say no to pizza," I say.

"I know."

At the town's main roundabout, around which dirty trucks spew fumes and dented cars jockey their way past insistent pedestrians, Sam and I sit outside a tired café with Euro leanings and have surprisingly good pizza.

After, I suggest looking for The Boys. Sam dismisses my idea, biting into his ice cream. Then, as a dirty white truck belching black exhaust plows through the roundabout blaring its horn at a mother pushing a baby stroller, Sam lets loose—"Sheeeeeeech!"

"I hope this lasts"

34 miles to Santiago

The mundane act of tying our shoes this morning carries with it a feeling of anticipation. That our feet have carried us across the width of Spain feels both improbable and undeniable. And now we're close, so close.

"I hope this lasts," Sam says, lifting one of his shoes. The sole has begun to come unglued; Sam is peeling it back to show me.

"Don't pull at it. You need those for a few more days."

"Think they'll make it to Finisterre?"

"They'll make it. Just don't mess with them."

We bought those shoes the day before we came to Spain. Sam tried on two different pairs of day hikers. Comparing them, he said, "These ones are slightly more comfortable, but these look so much cooler."

"Get the comfortable ones," I said without hesitation. "Especially since you didn't break them in."

"But, Dad, these ones—"

"You know what will be cool?" I interrupt. "Not getting blisters."

The young salesclerk, who had been helping us and listening to Sam's equivocation, chose this moment to chime in. "I hate to admit it," he said, "but your father is right."

"Yeah, but these ones are Chad." Sam grinned at him, holding up the more stylish pair.

The clerk raised his pierced eyebrow, pursed his lips, and nodded. "They are."

"They're your feet." I shrugged. "Get whichever ones you want."

"Don't worry," my son assured me. "I will."

He cradled the cool-looking pair. I went to find socks.

When Sam arrived at the checkout counter, he had the other, more comfortable shoes in his hand.

Grabbing my walking stick now, I turn to my son. "You glad you picked those shoes?"

"Oh, undoubtedly." Then hoisting his pack, Sam says, "I don't think I could have made the decision to get these ones over the others a moment earlier in life than I did."

"That's called growing up," I say. "You haven't had a single blister, have you?"

"No, sir." Sam spreads his arms wide. "I am The Chad supreme."

I push open the door. "Never mind what I said about growing up."

The air outside is cool, the sky gray. A low fog hangs close—it'll burn off within the hour. Galicia is notoriously wet, but we've seen little evidence of moody weather. Town is quick to quit, and corn grows between houses in the scraggy outskirts. Sam runs ahead to talk on the phone with one of his friends back home who is still awake in the middle of the night. Soon out of sight, I hear his voice, faint, and the occasional, "Sheeeeeeech." I lean into a steep incline, past mossy-trunked trees. In time, I no longer hear Sam at all. The trail drops. Large, hand-placed stepping-stones have been positioned across a flowing stream in an idyllic wood. I pass a small crossroads. A pine tree has become uprooted, its fall partially arrested by other trees around it. It leans over the trail at a precarious angle—what campers call, for obvious reasons, a widow-maker. Oak and chestnut trees have by now fully yielded their hold over the land to eucalyptus and pine. Then someone is running up from behind. Sam.

"I made a wrong turn," he says, gasping, laughing. "When I turned back, I saw you pass." Then he reaches into his pocket. "Look at this."

He swipes at his phone, then hands it to me.

"Oh my God." It's a photo of Taxicab Roger, standing naked beside a "100 km" marker. "Why is he doing that?" I ask.

Sam is hysterical with laughter.

"I can't unsee that," I say, shoving the phone back at Sam. "Why would he post that?"

"I love Roger," Sam says, still laughing.

"He must have jumped out of a cab to snap it." I shake my head and keep moving.

An attitude of looseness entered our walking back around O Cebreiro. It replaced the swagger that asserted itself near León, which had supplanted the sometimes-grim determination of the Meseta, which had succeeded the drive leading to Burgos, and the optimistic spring around Logroño, which had dispelled the hopeful trepidation of our start in Saint-Jean-Pied-du-Port. There's assurance in what we're doing now. In the value of it.

As I've grown older, I've become more and more aware of when I'm happy during the moment in which I am happy—and not merely in hindsight. Through all the grinding, the occasional battles, I have remained aware of the gift of this time. The knowledge that my son is ready to move out into the world, to begin his own life, is ever present in me. On this walk, not only has he been purging himself, but he has been making himself ready—discarding, observing, gathering. I, too, am making myself ready—gathering, observing, discarding. Knowing this, we keep walking.

Sam and I talk politeness, the sigma male, houseplants, steroids. Just outside the village of Castañeda, we pass a small stone house with a red wooden door, two tiny windows, and a slate roof with a chimney spewing smoke.

"I love that place," I tell Sam.

He looks over and, without hesitation, dismisses my fantasy out of hand. "The difference between that and a jail is a fireplace and a couch."

And that is the difference between my son and myself.

Viewing the world through the prism of fear dominated the first half of my life, and—as a result of my experience in the Meseta during my first Camino—the imperfect challenging of that fear has been a driving force of the second. I harbor no desires that it be otherwise—what I've learned, the insights gained, being able to identify fear playing such a part in others' lives—often unwittingly—has given me an awareness and perspective I would otherwise lack. But that my eldest son (and daughter) appear to be free of such fear is something for which I can only be grateful.

We stop at a hospitable bar and eat omelets made from eggs laid that morning and smell manure as we swill Cokes, then coffee. I decline Sam's offer of the morning ice cream cone.

We are firmly in dairy country now; apple trees line fields flush with cows. The land begins to roll, and Sam starts walking backward down a hill, talking nonsense about balancing his muscular exertion. I imagine him tripping and smashing his head or twisting an ankle so close to the end of our journey and being unable to finish. I say nothing. Shortly before noon, we cross the Puente de Ribadiso, built by the Romans in the sixth century over the Río Iso, and come upon James, sitting alone outside a café, sipping a glass of red wine.

I unsnap my pack and, letting it fall to the ground, take a seat across from him. We haven't seen our Camino fairy in days.

"Where you been, James?" Sam asks.

"I have just been walking seventy kilometers nonstop," he informs us.

"What?"

"There's been a beautiful moon," James says, as if this explains his days of nonstop walking.

"I've got something for you," Sam says, pulling out a fresh packet of loose tobacco I didn't know he was carrying. "Here." He offers James the pack.

"Oh, no, no," James says.

"Since I've bummed so many."

"You can roll me one, but I'm not taking your tobacco."

Sam has already begun to roll a cigarette.

"Let him give it to you, James," I say. Then I smile at our friend. "Just accept the love."

James looks at me, then at Sam, who hands the rolled cigarette over and begins to roll a second. "All right, give me that thing," he says.

Sam smiles and tosses him the packet. James begins to transfer the tobacco to his leather pouch. Several heaping handfuls later, he hands the packet back to Sam. "I saved you enough for a few."

"Cool," Sam says.

The two smokers smoke in silence. Then Sam gets up. "You want another glass of wine?" he calls over his shoulder.

"Sure," James calls back.

We watch Sam disappear through the hanging beads and into the bar. I return my attention to James. "Thanks. It was important to him, to give you that."

James nods. We sit. "I want to thank *you*," he says softly.

"For what?"

"For showing me what a father-son relationship can be."

I wave the remark away. "You don't see us when I'm trying to get him out of bed, or when I'm tired, or when he's hungry, or, or, or..."

"Just accept the love." James smiles, throwing my words back at me. "I've wanted to walk this with my son...so thank you."

I sit with his remark.

"You two talk about a lot, don't you?" he begins again.

"Everything and nothing. You try and sit Sam down for a chat and you won't get very far, but get him moving and it all comes out. And I've learned a lot on this trip, mostly to not have to have an answer or a solution for everything." We laugh. "It's for them to figure out, right? Setting him up in a certain way, to know he can trust himself, to know I'm behind him but to go out there. To go beyond us. That's the job, isn't it?"

Under normal circumstances—and despite the affection I feel for James—I'd be hesitant, even embarrassed, to be so unadorned and forthcoming with someone I know so lightly, but the Camino has done its work on me, burning away the normal protectiveness and encouraging the simplicity and power of directness and ownership of thoughts and feelings.

Sam returns with a glass of wine and a coffee for himself. "James, are you going to Finisterre?"

"I'm not sure what I'm doing yet," our friend says. "Are you?"

"Yeah, with Chris."

"You're not going?" James nods toward me.

"Santiago is enough for me," I say.

"Going beyond, is he?" James smiles at me.

"Going beyond." I smile back.

"Beyond what?" Sam asks.

I explain to Sam what James and I were discussing while he was gone.

"Whatever." Sam downs his coffee. "You ready?"

"You didn't get me a coffee, huh?"

"You didn't ask." Sam starts rolling another cigarette.

"Let's go." I rise and bend to get my pack.

"I'll see you gentlemen in Santiago," James says.

"I hope so." Sam offers James the cigarette.

James inspects the roll, then nods, impressed. "Thank you, Sam."

"A pleasure, James."

The trail dives deep into a lush wood, the path wide and worn by centuries. Eucalyptus trees shedding their bark line the way, perfuming the air. At kilometer marker 32, the sun burns through.

"Thirty-two, Dad! Sheeeeech!"

My grin comes fast. "Remember eight hundred?"

"The first one I remember noticing was seven ninety, at Roncesvalles."

In the tiny village of A Calle, we stop at a well-kept café. Sam orders three fried eggs. Then three more. "These things are very fresh," he says between heaping mouthfuls. By my count, my son has eaten a dozen eggs today.

Villages come more frequently now, and we pass through them without comment. It's late in the afternoon when we run into The Boys, Ryan and Chris, outside the town of O Pedrouzo, our stop for the night. And it's a good thing we do, since the village is slightly off the Camino, and we had begun to bypass it.

"You guys have a place reserved?" Chris asks.

"We do," I say. "Why?"

"The town is totally booked. We couldn't find a room."

"We're so close now, all the people," I say.

"Damn newbies," Sam says.

"We're just gonna walk all the way in tonight," Chris says.

"To Santiago?" Sam asks.

"It's only twenty k," Ryan says.

"Dad— -" There's excitement in Sam's voice.

"No way, Sammy. I'm tired. Santiago tomorrow."

The boys lead us into the town. We shake hands, confirming we'll reunite in Santiago, and they head off. We find our charmless-looking pension on the outskirts of the charmless town. As we enter, the woman behind the counter is turning away a young man looking for a room. I step up and announce our arrival, spelling our name. The woman hesitates, then looks down at her book. She flips a few pages. "Did you confirm your reservation?"

"What do you mean? Yes, I got a confirmation email."

Finally, she looks up. "But did you call and confirm?"

"No. But I have the confirmation here." I dig for my phone and try to find the email. I have records of thirty reservations and, as I begin to sense a problem, I find it difficult to locate the proper one.

"Well, we have no rooms left."

"No, I have a reservation. I paid."

"I have no record. If you didn't call to confirm…"

"Nowhere across the whole country has anyone asked us to call and confirm after I already have confirmation."

"We only hold rooms until five."

I look at my watch—5:15.

"So you just gave our room away fifteen minutes ago?"

"No—"

"So then—"

But the woman cuts me off and says something very fast that I don't catch.

It's said that the last thing one learns to communicate in a language is a sense of humor. But venting anger must be granted a special dispensation, and in this case, my disregard for mistakes is fueled by the Holy Trinity of righteousness, hunger, and exhaustion. I let loose with a torrent. Grammatically correct or not, my point is made in abundance. The woman behind the counter doesn't back down and comes at me just as hard. It's an ugly, unpleasant exchange.

The bottom line is that there is no room at the inn.

Storming up the street, I lift my hand to see trembling fingers. My rage has taken me off guard and frightened me. My old fear, that at the end of the day, I simply have no power; that I cannot take care of my son, or any of my children—fear that I have done so much to dispel—has reared its head as we are almost to the finish line. It feels, in this instant, that the rug has been pulled from my fantasy that I am, in fact, capable. Fear. Fear. I can only think of my father, and how this apple has not fallen as far from the tree as I have always maintained.

It took me decades to see my dad's rage as a misguided attempt to deal with the fear I only truly understood when he was on his deathbed.

I went to my dad while he was dying, after years of estrangement. His eyes betrayed him, his terror. I took his cool, now lizard-like, hand in mine. I wanted to let go but didn't. I sat with him. I apologized for not being the son he had wanted. I told him I loved him. When we were beyond words, we released our past—let it fall to rot on the ground where it belonged. More than a vestige of love remained.

I had gone to my father selfishly—and it must be said, at my wife's urging. I did so that I might be a better father to my own children. The gifts children bear us are complex.

Sam hurries to catch up. "Wow, Dad."

"I'm sorry, Sam. I shouldn't have spoken like that." I shake my head. "I've learned nothing."

"No, you were right."

"That doesn't matter."

We walk.

"Dad?"

"Yeah?"

"Your Spanish has gotten really good."

"Silence!"

The Camino Gods took mercy, and we found what was perhaps the last room in town. A lime-green box with torn curtains, frayed towels, and bed linen of dubious cleanliness. No matter. Today is the day we have been walking toward for the past thirty, and we're out long before sunup. On the edge of town, just before the trail plunges into the woods, a bread delivery truck races around a corner and nearly runs over Sam, who is walking in the middle of the previously deserted street. Some lessons aren't learned easily.

Once engulfed in the dense grove of giant eucalyptus trees, we find The Way already littered with flashlight beams moving in the herky-jerky rhythm of walkers. The clean, medicinal fragrance of the trees is strong in the dark. The moon, a day past full and still high, plays peek-a-boo through the canopy. The goal is to make Santiago by noon, for the pilgrim Mass. Sam has no interest in such a thing, and I only slightly more, but there are certain rituals in which a pilgrim traditionally partakes that I am eager to relive.

The Pórtico de la Gloria is the archway just inside the main western entrance of the Cathedral, carved in 1188 by Master Mateo—who, as his name implies, was a master of Romanesque sculpture. Tradition holds that arriving pilgrims lay their hand on the marble at the base of the Tree of Jesse (in essence, the family tree of Christ) carved into the central column. Millions of hands, over centuries, have worn deep grooves of five fingers into the marble, and grateful pilgrims have been known to drop and approach the portico on their knees. On my first Camino, I did just that. I've been wondering if I'll embarrass Sam and do the same this time.

Pilgrims then go around to the inside of the portico. Here, Mateo, in a mischievous move, carved himself into his masterpiece. It's believed that whoever touches their head to the head of the stone Mateo will be imbued with some of the master's genius. Next—and most memorable from my first trip—the pilgrim climbs the steps behind the high altar and, approaching from behind, embraces the jewel-encrusted statue of Saint James, giving thanks for safe passage on the Camino and offering prayers for those who helped along the way. Naturally, Sam shows little interest when I mention such chores that await us today.

In a clearing, we see a glow over the horizon—Santiago. We quicken our pace. The night begins to fold back on itself, and I become conscious of how impossible it seems, and then how inevitable, how quick and profound, the change from darkness to light so often is.

The trail begins to climb, and a high buzzing sound starts to grow. The path skirts the Santiago airport, and a lone jet, its engines whining, readies itself on the runway before takeoff. Sam and I are talking the difference between buddies and friends, and then altruism, and then Sam concludes, "Being kind is kind of sick."

"Well put, Sam," I say.

On the steep climb to Monte do Gozo, the hilltop from which the spires of the Cathedral are first visible, and from where Pope John Paul II once said Mass, Sam stops and flexes his leg. "My left knee is complaining," he says. Then looking down at his bent limb, screams out, "Silence!"

Nearby walkers turn to look.

"You know, if you scream like that, most people think you're crazy," he says. "I'm not crazy."

I scream as well.

"Not bad, Dad." Sam smiles. "Not great, but not bad."

As we approach the suburbs, the trail/path/Way/road is filled with a seemingly endless stream of people. Many have light day packs, some have no packs at all. A woman pushes a man in a wheelchair; a small boy walks beside her carrying a large butterfly net. Older couples march with determination. Teens whoop and holler. Long-haul pilgrims stride with confidence. Gone is any resentment over newbies or interlopers to the trail. "All these people," Sam says, "this is so cool." He begins to sing Bruce Springsteen's "The Promised Land," loudly.

Mister I ain't a boy, no I'm a man
And I believe in a promised land.

We broach the outer city, through roundabouts and across intersections. The mass of walkers begins to dissipate among city life. We stop for coffee. Then, ten minutes later, we stop again, this time for a breakfast plate of jamón ibérico. We're hungry, sure, but really, we just don't want it to end.

When we enter the old town, I need to find a bathroom and go into a café. The place is empty. The man behind the bar refuses me use of the toilet unless I buy something. I order a Coke and when I return, a warm can is sitting on the bar.

"*Cuanto cuesta?*" I ask.

"One fifty," the man spits out.

I toss a two-euro coin on the bar beside the untouched can and walk out.

It takes an active effort to dismiss my resentment of the man. He serves only as a reminder that life beyond the Camino is still spinning, that all our efforts over the past five hundred miles exist in and of and for themselves. There is no reward, no special dispensation from the wider world awaiting us.

As has happened so often along the way, we lose the yellow arrows amid the city chaos. The first time I arrived in Santiago, I got lost coming in, until a young man who had been panhandling for money took it upon himself to grab me by the arm and lead me through the streets to the Cathedral. This time, Sam and I are led by a kind of inner gravity. We weave left and right through the narrow streets and lanes without equivocation. We're up over a rise and then the cobbled road begins to descend and we're passing through an arch and then we're emerging into a vast open square and then there it is—the Cathedral.

"Sheeeeeeech!"

I embrace Sam. Then I hug him again.

The Romanesque church was consecrated in 1211, the baroque facade, capped by a statue of Saint James clad in pilgrim garb, added in the eighteenth century. Praza do Obradoiro, the open plaza in front of the Cathedral, is the unspoken meeting place for pilgrims. Dozens hang around, chatting, laughing, scanning for friends, resting, sleeping, using backpacks for pillows.

"Wow," I repeat dumbly, looking around.

We don't know what to do. Our excitement is too great to allow us to focus. The gate at the base of the steps leading to the Pórtico de la Gloria is locked.

"Let's go around back. It must be open there to let people in," I suggest.

In the Praza da Quintana, the line to get into the Cathedral is too long and has been capped for the day. We take a seat at a café and look up at the ornately carved eastern facade above the Door of Pardon.

Sam slumps. "I'm tired," he confesses. I haven't heard him admit fatigue since Roncesvalles.

We order Coke and coffee. I go into the bathroom and, as the door locks behind me, I'm surprised by a burst of sobs. Relief, sadness, joy, somehow disappointment, confusion, exhaustion, exhilaration, comingle— the awful truth of the sweetness of life throbs in an unguarded mix of emotions.

Back outside, neither of us is satisfied to sit long. We get up and walk back around to the front of the Cathedral. We find The Boys, Ryan and Chris, just waking from a nap after their long night of walking. And there are The White People, scrubbed and showered, having gotten in the day before. Alex and Morgan drift up as well, Morgan seeming so remote as to appear almost translucent. Then suddenly there's James, stepping lightly. When a taxi stops in the corner of the square, Sam lets out a shout: "Roger!"

We all share hugs and snap photos.

When I approach a guard, he tells me that it's no longer possible to lay a hand on the Tree of Jesse, erosion having taken its toll. Nor is it allowed to touch one's head to Mateo's, for the same reason. Even hugging the statue of the patron saint is off-limits for now. Without the rituals to punctuate our journey, I feel lost. I stand dazed, vibrating.

Seeing me staring off glassy-eyed, Sam leaves our friends and walks over.

"You all right?" he asks.

"Yeah." I choke back emotion again. Then, trying to gather myself, "Everything's locked," I tell him. "Can't even hug the saint."

My son puts a paternal arm around my shoulder. "It's OK, Dad. This one truly was about the journey."

"Ten out of ten"

After my feet are up the wall for a half hour, and while Sam is flooding the bathroom in his usual fashion, I head out to find where his trail for the morning begins. I'm glad I do. The markers for Finisterre are difficult to locate, and I follow them to a park at the western edge of town. I'm late getting back, and Sam is already having drinks with the gang.

The next morning, we're up long before daylight but are still a half hour late to meet Chris in front of the Cathedral. He is just walking up as we arrive. To my thinking, this does not bode well for the two of them making a three-day walk in two days—but I say nothing. I lead them down Rua des Hortas to Rue da Poza de Bar and to the western edge of town. In Carballeira de San Lourenzo, beneath lush trees shadowing the already dark predawn, we nearly miss the small column I located yesterday, pointing the way toward the coast. I take a badly out-of-focus picture in the blackness, hug Sam, and quietly ask Chris to keep him out of the road. I watch them round a bend and disappear into a tunnel in the dark, and they're gone.

Not since childhood, walking home from school each afternoon, do I recall a similar feeling of aloneness. I spend the morning drifting around town. I walk up into Parque Alameda and view the Cathedral from a high vantage. I loiter in a Spanish version of a Venetian café. I check my phone and see that I have walked well over a million steps in the past month. And I allow myself only a single glance per hour at the newly installed tracking app with which I'm following Sam and Chris's progress. Occasionally, I get a live feed of exactly where they are; more often, the screen appears gray and I'm confronted with the words, *Moving near Galicia.*

Just off Praza do Obradoiro, a long line in front of a nondescript building snakes around the corner and down the block. Inside is where those who have traversed the country present their fully stamped pilgrim passports and receive the Compostela, sanctioned proof of completion of the Camino de Santiago. I have both Sam and my passports and take a spot in line. When I finally get inside, I may as well be at the Spanish version of the DMV. It's chaos. Large fans in the corners blow hot air. A long and high counter separates fifteen harried clerks from the hundreds of hungry pilgrims. People are shouting and jostling. It is a distant cry from my first Camino, when I sauntered up a flight of stairs to a dark room where an old man waited, alone and eager to certify my walk.

I watch the screen for my number and finally approach the counter. The woman to whom I hand Sam and my passports takes them without glancing up. She begins the paperwork and in time raises her eyes.

"Which one is Sam? Wait, where's the other person?"

I begin to explain that Sam is walking to Finisterre and won't have time to come here after he returns before our early flight. Long before I'm finished, she's handing me back the passports.

"Each person needs to bring their own."

"But I just explained. He's my son. We walked together—"

She's having none of it. I ask to speak with a supervisor. She too is uninterested in my story. I stand slack-jawed until the woman behind the counter calls, "Next," and two freshly showered pilgrims, each carrying their own passports, shoulder me aside.

I wasn't particularly interested in the Compostela; the stamped passport itself is a much more worthy reminder of the time committed and distance covered. But I feel briefly unseen, as if our efforts have been discounted. Still, I know neither their words nor their refusal to validate our walk mean anything.

I return to the square in front of the Cathedral. Two dozen over-fifty walkers traveling as a group arrive. There are photos, raised walking sticks, smiles. The group mingles, people hug, mingle some more, in some cases reencounter a person they've previously hugged and, laughing, hug them again. Small groups cluster and talk and take more photos, but my attention is drawn to those who eventually stand quietly and stare off.

I see it over and over. With each new arrival, after the war whoops and high fives, there comes the moment when that stare overtakes them.

While we all walk the same route—millions of us over the centuries—no one walks the same Camino. In a very real way, this trip is a private one. And a silent reckoning needs to be made. It may take days, weeks—and in my case, there were things that did not come clear to me, lessons learned that were not understood, for years after my first walk. Like The Way itself, the gifts of the Camino unfold slowly. I know this. I am in no rush today.

All the while I sit, the thought of Sam wandering out into the road without me to yell/guide him back is never far from my mind. Parenting never rests.

Tomorrow, I'll take a taxi and go out to Finisterre. It will take me less than an hour to drive what Sam and Chris will walk in two brutally long days. I will wait by mile marker zero on the cliff above the white birds that bob in the sea beside the small fishing boats that rest on its placid surface. The late-day sun will reflect off the water. I'll watch as my son comes marching up the final hill, legs pumping, arms swinging free, shirt off, skin red, a broad grin on his face. He'll throw his arms open wide, and I'll receive him. I'll take the boys' picture. I'll give them the food I've brought, and they'll sit and eat and stare out, proud and too excited yet to be tired. Finally, we'll get back in the taxi, the sun setting directly behind us as we drive, filling the car with a golden, blessed light. Later that night, I'll hear Sam singing in the shower, a single line from a song, over and over—"The single life ain't so bad." Then he'll ask me to accompany him as he takes his tattered shoes and leaves them at the base of the stairs in front of the great Cathedral. I'll watch as he crouches over them, silent for a moment, head bowed. The next morning at the airport, we'll sit across a small table drinking orange juice, and Sam will reach out his hand to shake mine. He will look at me and say, "Dad, that's the only ten-out-of-ten thing I've ever done in my life." As he removes his hand, he'll knock over my orange juice. And we'll laugh.

But for now, I sit in the square, watching pilgrims arrive after their arduous trek across Spain. The euphoria, the relief, the not knowing what to do next, the eventual staring off. Four young women in their twenties arrive. Soon, they are all on the verge of tears, staring up at the Cathedral, the bewildered look on their faces that says, "Is this it? What now?" I want to approach them and tell them I understand. I want to begin again, to go back to Saint-Jean-Pied-de-Port and eat pizza at that first café and have Sam shatter a glass as he gets up. I want to see his giddy excitement that first morning as he puts on his pack and grins. I want to drag him out of bed each day, I want to be tortured by that damn Australian accent one more time. I want to go back to those damn parent/teacher conferences and properly defend my son. I want to watch those endless karate classes one more time. I want a redo on his birth. I want all of it again.

They're setting up a stage in the middle of the square now—a bicycle race is finishing here tomorrow. Preparations are underway. Banners and flags are being placed. Life is moving forward.

I look up at the Cathedral: the sun has briefly gone behind the statue of Saint James, clothed in the pilgrim's long cloak and hat and staff, crowning the facade high up. Rays of light blast out from either side of him. *Thank you* is all I can think, and so I say it aloud. The words feel insufficient, as so many prayers do. They are all I have. I say them again. "Thank you."

Acknowledgments

Jack Hitt's recounting of his Camino in *Off the Road* inspired me to take the walk that changed my life decades ago. That I owe so much to someone I've never met is a testament to the power of books. I'm deeply indebted to some early readers of this manuscript—my high school English teacher and oldest friend, Eddie Vanston, Spain aficionado Lisa Abend, and Camino veteran Dan Wilhelm. All gave more of themselves than they needed to. I bow down to them. David Kuhn was, as always, direct, clear, and solution oriented. I'm very grateful to have him in my corner. Nate Mancuso was likewise attuned and needs acknowledgment.

Immense gratitude is directed to the folks at Grand Central. Ben Sevier and Colin Dickerman deserve my thanks. Suzanne O'Neill is so supportive an editor, and such a pleasure to work with, that I almost didn't notice how she kept pushing for more—almost. There would be no book without her. My deepest gratitude. Much thanks to Jeff Holt for carefully overseeing the production process. Big thank-you to Anne Newgarden for her detailed and discreet copy edit. A very large thank-you to Liz Connor for her imaginative cover art and willingness to indulge a nosy author in the process. And to the design team at Jouve for the lovely interior design. Much appreciation to Jimmy Franco in publicity and Janine Perez in marketing. Huge and affectionate thanks to Jacqueline Young, who kept things on track with a nudge and a smile.

Massive thanks always to Brian Liebman and Cory Richman. Jill

Fritzo and her team, Stephen Fertelmes and Jennifer Sandler, are tireless and passionate and must be acknowledged.

Thank-yous and a lot beside that are owed to "my favorite kid," Willow, for helping me "keep it real," and to the mighty Rowan. The walk and book—and so much more—could simply not have happened without Dolores. My love. And thanks must of course go to Sam—for sharing himself with me and allowing me to share him with you. Not every nineteen-year-old would consent to spending his summer on the hoof with the old man. My life is richer for the experience.

About the Author

Andrew McCarthy is the author of three books in addition to *Walking with Sam*: *Brat: An '80s Story*, *Just Fly Away*, and *The Longest Way Home*—all *New York Times* bestsellers. He is an award-winning travel writer and served for a dozen years as an editor-at-large at *National Geographic Traveler* magazine. Best known as an actor for the past four decades, Andrew has appeared in such iconic films as *Pretty in Pink* and *Less Than Zero*. He lives in New York.